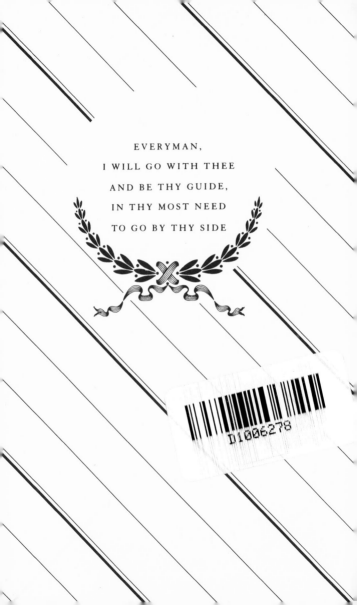

EVERYMAN,
I WILL GO WITH THEE
AND BE THY GUIDE,
IN THY MOST NEED
TO GO BY THY SIDE

Zen Poems

Selected and edited by
Peter Harris

EVERYMAN'S LIBRARY

POCKET POETS

Alfred A. Knopf · New York · Toronto

THIS IS A BORZOI BOOK

PUBLISHED BY ALFRED A. KNOPF, INC.

This selection by Peter Harris first published in
Everyman's Library, 1999

Copyright © 1999 by David Campbell Publishers Ltd.

A list of acknowledgments to copyright owners can be found at the back of
this volume.

All rights reserved under International and Pan-American Copyright
Conventions. Published in the United States by Alfred A. Knopf, Inc., New
York, and simultaneously in Canada by Random House of Canada Limited,
Toronto. Distributed by Random House, Inc., New York

ISBN 0-375-40552-6
LC 98-54776

Library of Congress Cataloging-in-Publication Data
Zen poems / selected and edited by Peter Harris.
p.   cm.—(Everyman's library pocket poets)
Includes index.
ISBN 0-375-40552-6 (alk. paper)
1. Zen poetry, Chinese—Translations into English.   2. Zen poetry,
Japanese—Translations into English.   3. Zen poetry,
Korean—Translations into English.   4. Zen poetry—Translations into
English.   I. Harris. Peter, 1947– .   II. Series.
PL2658.E3Z45   1999   98-54776
808.81′9382943927—dc21   CIP

Typography by Peter B. Willberg

Typeset in the UK by AccComputing, Castle Cary, Somerset

Printed and bound in Germany by
Graphischer Grossbetrieb Pössneck GmbH

CONTENTS

11

FOREWORD

What is Zen poetry? You could argue that it is poetry by Zen monks. You could define it as all the poetry written by people influenced by Zen. Or you could just treat any poems with a feeling of Zen about them as Zen poetry.

The simplest definition is the first one: that it is poetry by Zen monks, especially in the countries where Zen has a long history – China, Japan, Korea and Vietnam. (Zen is a Japanese word that derives from the Chinese term Chan. Chan is a transliteration of the Sanskrit word *dhyana*, meditation, attesting to Zen's ultimate origins in India.)

But that definition really isn't enough. An anthology restricted to the poetry of Zen monks would miss out a great deal, and include much that was irrelevant. Zen monks wrote poems about a wide variety of experiences, not all of them to do with Zen by any means. (There are a few poems of this kind in this anthology – for example, the Zen monk Chugan Engetsu's poem about getting malaria in China.) Moreover many Zen monks – the Japanese poet Sogi, for example – were Zen in name but not really in practice. Then again, Zen is only one among a variety of Buddhist beliefs; and some of the Chinese and Japanese poets we think of as writing with true Zen

Buddhist insight actually belonged to some other sect than Zen.

On the other hand, some brilliant lay poets in China and Japan owed part of their inspiration to Zen, without having devoted their entire lives to it either as monks or recluses. Several leading Chinese poets of the Tang and Song dynasties, among them Wang Wei and Su Dongpo, were strongly drawn to Zen ideas, and wrote a good deal of poetry in a Zen mode, though without regarding themselves as Zen poets as such. Many others – the lyricist Bai Juyi, for example – also sympathized deeply with Zen, but as a solace in times of adversity and as part of a broader stream of philosophical interests rather than as an exclusive creed.

The same is true of some of the most accomplished poets of Japan. Most people accept that one of Japan's finest poets, Basho, was influenced by Zen, but clearly it was not his only source of inspiration. To perfect the art of writing hokku or haiku, the short allusive verses so often connected with his name, Basho also drew extensively on other poetic traditions. (Other masters of hokku, Buson and Issa for instance, were even less closely associated with Zen than Basho; and the view that hokku and Zen are two sides of the same coin is quite misleading.)

Having said all that, I should add that a number of remarkable poets in China and Japan were indeed Zen monks or people who led a reclusive existence. In China the best known of them is Hanshan, "Cold Mountain". Like other Chinese poets with an interest in Buddhism, Hanshan was a strong influence on later generations of Zen monk poets in Japan, including the remarkable poet-recluse Ryokan. Many of these Japanese monk poets belonged to a system of state-supported monasteries that went by the collective name of Gozan, "the Five Mountains"; and Five Mountain poets are sometimes portrayed as being at the heart of the Zen poetic tradition.

As well as its other influences, Zen had an important formative influence on the way many Chinese and Japanese poets thought about writing poetry. The Chinese poet Yang Wanli, for example, believed that there was a strong connection between the sudden enlightenment of Zen as he understood it and a sudden awakening of the poet to the true art of poetry. Yang wrote his own best poems – few of them explicitly associated with Zen, but many of them paradoxical or slightly bizarre – after experiencing just such an awakening. And in his unorthodox use of language the Japanese monk Shinkei seems to have reflected a Zen-like sense of how words should be used to convey the ambiguities of perception.

In this anthology I have tried to include poems reflecting all these facets of Zen. The poets are arranged chronologically so that the major poets like Wang Wei and Hanshan can be sampled at some length. The Five Mountain poets are, if anything, over-represented, and overall I have included fewer poets than I would have liked, largely because of what is available in readable translation.

There are a few poems included here because I am particularly fond of the poets concerned, even though they are only marginally connected with Zen. They include poets who lived too early to be Zen devotees (such as Xie Lingyun, the first poet in the book), or disqualify themselves for some other reason, but who wrote poems with a tangible Zen mood to them.

There is one kind of Zen poetry that is not given much space here. I am referring to the devotional hymns (*gatha*) and more technical theological verses that make up a good deal of Buddhist literature. These are often quite hard to understand without extensive glosses, and tend to be wooden, especially in English. I have included just a few instances of the more technical poems, mostly ones by Su Dongpo, to give some idea of what they are like.

Purists might argue that writings inspired by Zen are ultimately a contradiction in terms. After all, Zen is a means of achieving sudden enlightenment by breaking with the constraints of commentary and tradition, and by transcending the bounds of language. Fortunately for us, not even the most enlightened poets in this collection achieved this degree of purity (though one or two came close). Indeed what is striking about most of the poets included here, including the monks, is their talkativeness, the variety of their moods, and their readiness to temper their higher aspirations with everyday human concerns.

Zen has something of a reputation for remoteness, one that derives partly from the famous "koans" or riddles – "what is the sound of one hand clapping?" – with which Japanese Zen masters provoke their pupils. The humanity of many of the poems in this collection make them more accessible than this reputation allows. They give us, I think, a feeling for the vivid, immediate qualities of Zen that more rarified, exalted writings could not convey.

Peter Harris
Wellington, New Zealand
September 1998

A note about Chinese names in English: I have used the standard pinyin *form of romanization for names of authors and names in the titles of poems, but to keep translations intact I have left names in the actual texts of poems untouched. This has resulted in minor inconsistencies which I hope are not too obtrusive.*

My thanks to Duncan Campbell, Julian Chapple, Chong-wha Chung, Stephen Epstein and Hongkey Yoon for their generous help and advice.

ZEN POEMS

Written on the Lake on my Way Back to the Retreat at Stone Cliff

Between dusk and dawn the weather is constantly
     changing,
Bathing mountain and lake alike in radiant sunlight.
This radiant sunlight filled me with such joy,
That lost in delight I quite forgot to go home.
When I left my valley the day had scarcely broken,
When I stepped into my boat the light was growing
     dim.
Forest and gorge were veiled in sombre colours,
The sunset clouds mingled with evening haze.
Gay panoply of water-chestnut, lotus,
Rushes and cattails growing side by side,
I swept them aside with my hands as I hastened
     southwards.
How glad I was to reach my house in the east!
Once the mind stops striving the world loses
     importance,
Once the heart is content it does not swerve from the
     truth.
I send these words to those who would nurture their
     lives:
Try using this Method if you want the Truth.

XIE LINGYUN   25
TR. J. D. FRODSHAM

On Climbing the Highest Peak of Stone Gate

At dawn with staff in hand I climbed the crags,
At dusk I made my camp among the mountains.
Only a few peaks rise as high as this house,
Facing the crags, it overlooks winding streams.
In front of its gates a vast forest stretches,
While boulders are heaped round its very steps.
Hemmed in by mountains, there seems no way out,
The track gets lost among the thick bamboos.
My visitors can never find their way,
And when they leave, forget the path they took.
The raging torrents rush on through the dusk,
The monkeys clamour shrilly through the night.
Deep in meditation, how can I part from Truth?
I cherish the Way and never will swerve from it.
My heart is one with the trees of late autumn,
My eyes delight in the buds of early spring.
I dwell with my constant companions and wait for
    my end,
Content to find peace through accepting the flux
    of things.
I only regret that there is no kindred soul,
To climb with me this ladder to the clouds in the blue.

XIE LINGYUN

TR. J. D. FRODSHAM

Setting out at Night from the Pavilion at Stone Pass

I've travelled round the hills for hundreds of miles,
Afloat on a stream at dusk these last ten days.
When the birds head home I give the oars a rest;
As the stars grow faint I order us on our way.
High and clear the moon shines bright at dawn;
Cold and wet the morning dewdrops form.

On Founding a Retreat for the Sangha at Stone Cliff

Round the city's four walls He saw men's suffering,
That through Three Periods never knows an end.
Ephemeral joys darkened the eyes of men,
Yet His deep insight understood it all.
When we are young we fret that time goes slowly,
As we grow old decay comes on apace.
So swiftly this deceiving dream is over,
That sudden as storm or lightning once arose.
I knew that my good karma was not ended,
But time was flying past and would not stay.
Sincerely I copy His actions on Vulture Peak,
Remembering the rules He gave in Jetavana.
A waterfall goes flying past the courtyard,
A lofty forest dazzles at the window.
In this house of meditation we realize all is void,
In this temple of debate we analyse subtle truths.

TR. J. D. FRODSHAM

The body is the Bodhi tree,
The mind is like a clear mirror.
At all times we must strive to polish it,
And must not let the dust collect
>Shenxiu, according to Huineng,
>the sixth Patriarch of Zen

Bodhi originally has no tree
The mirror also has no stand.
Buddha nature is always clear and pure;
Where is there room for dust?

I originally came to China
to transmit the teaching and save deluded beings.
One flower opens five petals,
and the fruit ripens of itself.
>   Bodhidharma, according to
>   Huineng

If evil flowers bloom in the mind-ground,
Five blossoms flower from the stem.
Together they will create the karma of ignorance;
Now the mind-ground is blown by the winds of karma.

If correct flowers bloom in the mind-ground,
Five blossoms flower from the stem.
Together practise the *prajna* wisdom;
In the future this will be the enlightenment of
     the Buddha.

Deluded, a Buddha is a sentient being;
Awakened, a sentient being is a Buddha.
Ignorant, a Buddha is a sentient being;
With wisdom, a sentient being is a Buddha.
If the mind is warped, a Buddha is a sentient being;
If the mind is impartial, a sentient being is a Buddha.
When once a warped mind is produced,
Buddha is concealed within the sentient being.
If for one instant of thought we become impartial,
Then sentient beings are themselves Buddha.
In our mind itself a Buddha exists,
Our own Buddha is the true Buddha.
If we do not have in ourselves the Buddha mind,
Then where are we to seek Buddha?

HUINENG   31
TR. PHILIP YAMPOLSKY

Enjoying the Cool

Tall trees—more than ten thousand trunks:
A pure flow threading through their midst.
Ahead, above the mouth of the great river
Clear and free comes a distant wind.
Flowing ripples dampen the white sand;
White sturgeon seem to swim in the void.
I lie down upon a large flat rock;
Rising billows cleanse my humble body.
I rinse my mouth and then wash my feet,
And face an old fisherman in front of me.
Greedy for bait—how many altogether?
Vain thoughts, east of the lotus leaves.

TR. PAULINE YU

An Autumn Evening in the Hills

Through empty hills new washed by rain
As dusk descends the autumn comes;
Bright moonlight falls through pines,
Clear springs flow over stones;
The bamboos rustle as girls return from washing,
Lotus flowers stir as a fishing boat casts off;
Faded the fragrance of spring,
Yet, friend, there is enough to keep you here.

Seeking a Night's Lodging at the Monastery
of the Chan Master Daoyi

The master of unity lodges on Taibo Mountain,
A lofty peak emerging from clouds and mist.
Chanting flows everywhere through ravines;
The flower's rain is only on one peak.
His tracks because of no-mind are concealed;
His name is known because of his instruction.
When birds arrive he speaks of the Dharma again;
When guests depart he meditates in peace once more.
By daylight he walks to the end of dewy pines,
In the evening sleeping next to the monastery.
His innermost chamber hidden in deep bamboo,
On a clear night he listens to distant streams.
Before this was just amid misty clouds:
Today it is in front of my pillow and mat.
How can I stay just for a while?
I should render service for an entire life.

      TR. PAULINE YU

THE WANG RIVER COLLECTION
[a series of twenty poems about Wang Wei's country retreat near the Wang River]

Meng Wall Hollow

A new home by a gap in the Meng wall—
Of the old trees, a few gnarled willows are left.
Those who come in future, who will they be,
Grieving in vain for what others had before?

Huazi Ridge

Birds fly away to the ends of the earth;
The mountains have an autumn look again.
Going up Huazi Ridge, and coming down,
I am moved by feelings of the utmost sorrow.

Grainy Apricot Lodge

We cut grainy apricot wood for beams,
And bind sweet-smelling thatch for the eaves.
I do not know if the clouds among the rafters
Will go to make rain among men.

Fine Bamboo Mountain Range

Sleek stems reflected in empty winding waters;
Dark green and emerald, floating on gentle ripples—
Secretly we take the Mount Shang track
Without the woodcutters knowing.

Deer Enclosure

In the empty mountain no one to be seen,
Only the distant sound of people's voices.
The evening sun enters the deep wood,
Shining again on dark green moss.

Magnolia Enclosure

The autumn hills hold back the last of the light;
Birds fly past, chasing companions up ahead.
Rich emerald greens, at times distinct and clear—
The evening mist has no place to settle.

Ailanthus Bank

They bear a fruit that's red and also green,
And then they bloom a second time, like flowers.
In the hills I entertain my guests
By setting out these cups of ailanthus.

Pagoda-Tree Footpath

The narrow path is shaded by pagoda-trees,
its dark shadows a mass of green moss.
The gatekeeper still sweeps it clean in welcome,
worried in case a monk from the hills comes by.

Lakeside Pavilion

A light boat greets the arriving guest,
Coming over the lake from far away.

Across the gallery we raise our cups;
On every side the lotus is in bloom.

The Southern Cottage

Towards the Southern Cottage the skiff goes;
the Northern Cottage is distant, hard to reach.
Over there on shore I make out people's homes—
Too far away for us to recognize each other.

Lake Yi

Playing flutes we reach the distant shore;
At sunset I see you on your way.
Back on the lake, with a turn of the head I see
Dark mountain green unfurling white clouds.

Willow Waves

*[Twigs from the willow, the word for which in Chinese
sounds the same as the word for "stay", were offered by
friends on parting]*

Row on row, unbroken, gossamer willows
Their images inverted into the clear ripples.
A study of those on royal moat—yet not,
For there the spring winds bring the pain of parting.

Luan Family Rapids

The wind howls in the autumn rain,
The water flows swiftly over the stones.

Jumping waves smack into one another;
White herons start up in fright, then drop down again.

Gold Dust Spring

Drink daily from Gold Dust Spring,
and have a thousand years or more of youth.
Blue phoenixes will whirl your dappled dragons
      upwards;
In plumes and feathers you'll attend the Jade
      Emperor's court.

White Pebble Rapids

Clear shallow water, White Pebble Rapids,
Green rushes sturdy enough to grasp.
Families live east and west of the water,
Wash their silk under the bright moon.

The Northern Cottage

By the Northern Cottage to the north of the lakewater,
Trees intermingled dapple the red balustrades.
The Southern River's waters meander through,
Lit up, then lost, on the edges of the black forest.

Bamboo District Lodge

Sitting alone among secluded bamboos
I play the zither, whistle on and on;
Deep in the woods, unknown to the world,
A bright moon comes and shines on me.

Lily Magnolia Hollow

On the tips of branches, hibiscus flowers
In the hills bear petals cased in red;
Down by the stream, by the deserted house,
They bloom in profusion, then fall to earth.

Lacquer Tree Grove

*[The poet Guo Pu once called the Daoist philosopher
Zhuangzi "proud" for serving as an official in charge of a
lacquer tree orchard]*

That man of old was not a proud official:
He had had no experience of the world's affairs,
And so by chance took on a minor posting,
His charge an inanimate cluster of trees.

Pepper Garden

With cup of cinnamon I greet the son of god,
Pollia I give as a gift to the fair one;
Pepper libations I make to the jade mat—
Let my lord come down from among the clouds!

In my Lodge at Wang Chuan after a Long Rain

The woods have stored the rain, and slow comes
    the smoke
As rice is cooked on faggots and carried to the fields;
Over the quiet marsh-land flies a white egret,
And mango-birds are singing in the full summer
    trees...
I have learned to watch in peace the mountain
    morning-glories,
To eat split dewy sunflower-seeds under a bough
    of pine,
To yield the post of honour to any boor at all...
Why should I frighten sea-gulls, even with a thought?

    TR. WITTER BYNNER

Light Lines on a Flat Rock

Dear flat rock
        facing the stream

Where the willows are sweeping
        over my wine cup again

If you say that the spring wind
        has no understanding

Why should it come blowing me
        these falling flowers?

Green Creek

To get right down to Yellow Flower River
I often follow the waters of Green Creek.
They wind around the mountains endlessly—
A path straight there would run a few score miles.

There are sounds of water crashing on tumbled stones;
Scenes of silence deep within the pines.
Water chestnut and water fringe float on the ripples;
Still limpid waters mirror the reeds.

My mind is unencumbered, at its ease now,
Clear and tranquil, as the river is.
Come, stay a while, rest here upon this stone—
Cast out a fishing line, and let things be.

TR. PETER HARRIS

Suffering from the Heat

Red sun filled sky and earth
Clouds of fire massed into mountains
Vegetation all burnt and shrivelled up
Rivers and lakes all quite dry

Lightest silk felt too heavy to wear
Densest trees gave only wretched shade
Straw mats were unapproachable
Linen was washed three times a day

My thoughts went out of the world
To somewhere utterly alone
Far winds came from a thousand miles
Rivers and seas washed impurities away
Now I realized, the body is the affliction
At last I knew, my mind has never awakened
Here is the way to Nirvana, the gate
To pass through to the joy of purity.

Living in the Hills: Impromptu Verses

I close my brushwood door in solitude
And face the vast sky as late sunset falls.
The pine trees: cranes are nesting all around.
My wicker gate: a visitor seldom calls.
The tender bamboo's dusted with fresh powder.
Red lotuses strip off their former bloom.
Lamps shine out at the ford, and everywhere
The water-chestnut pickers wander home.

Stone Gate Monastery on Mount Lantian

In the setting sun, mountains and waters were lovely.
The tossing boat trusted the home-blowing wind.
Enjoying the strangeness, unaware of distance,
I followed all the way to the source of the spring.
Afar I loved the lushness of clouds and trees;
At first I thought the route was not the same.
How could I know the clear flow turned?
Suddenly I passed through the mountain ahead.
I left the boat and readied my light staff,
Truly satisfied with what I encountered:
Old monks—four or five men,
At leisure in the shade of pine and cypress.
At morning chants the forest has not yet dawned;
During night meditation, mountains are even stiller.
Their minds of the Tao reach to shepherd boys;
They ask a woodman about worldly affairs.
At night they lodge beneath the tall forest;
Burning incense, they sleep on clean white mats.
The valley stream's fragrance pervades men's clothes;
The mountain moon illumines the stone walls.
Seeking again I fear I'd lose the way;
Tomorrow I will go out to continue my climb.
Smiling I'll leave the men of Peach Blossom Spring:
When blossoms are red I will come to see them again.

Visiting the Forest Pavilion of the Recluse, Cui Xingzong,
with Lu Xiang

The green trees give layers of shade
     in all directions

The green moss thickens daily
     and so there is no dust

He sits legs outstretched hair unkempt
     under the tall pines

And regards with the whites of his eyes
     the rest of the world

  TR. G. W. ROBINSON

Farm House on the Wei Stream

The slanting sun shines on the cluster of small houses
    upon the heights.
Oxen and sheep are coming home along the distant
    lane.
An old countryman is thinking of the herd-boy,
He leans on his staff by the thorn-branch gate,
    watching,
Pheasants are calling, the wheat is coming into ear,
Silkworms sleep, the mulberry-leaves are thin.
Labourers, with their hoes over their shoulders, arrive;
They speak pleasantly together, loth to part.
It is for this I long—unambitious peace!
Disappointed in my hopes, dissatisfied, I hum
    "Dwindled and Shrunken".

In the Hills

White rocks jutting from Ching stream
The weather's cold, red leaves few
No rain at all on the paths in the hills
Clothes are wet with the blue air.

Weeping for Ying Yao

We send you home to a grave on Stone Tower
    Mountain;
through the green green of pine and cypress,
    mourners' carriages return.
Among white clouds we've laid your bones—it is
    ended forever;
only the mindless waters remain, flowing down to the
    world of men.

Zhongnan Retreat

In middle age I'm quite drawn to the Way.
Here by the hills I've built my home. I go
—Whenever the spirit seizes me—alone
To see the spots that other folk don't know.
I walk to the head of the stream, sit down, and watch
For when the clouds rise. On the forest track
By chance I meet an old man, and we talk
And laugh, and I don't think of going back.

Lines

You who have come from my old country,
Tell me what has happened there!—
Was the plum, when you passed my silken window,
Opening its first cold blossom?

On Missing my Way to the Monastery of Heaped Fragrance

I cannot find the Monastery of Heaped Fragrance,
Miles up now
   into the clouds of the summit.
There is no footpath through the ancient woods.
Where did the bell sound, deep in the mountain?
The voice of the torrent gulps over jagged stones;
Sunlight hardly warms the bluish pines.
As dusk deepens in these unfathomable mazes,
I practise meditation
   to subdue the dragon of desire.

   TR. INNES HERDAN

Sitting Alone on an Autumn Night

I sit alone sad at my whitening hair
Waiting for ten o'clock in my empty house
In the rain the hill fruits fall
Under the lamp grasshoppers sound
White hairs will never be transformed
That elixir is beyond creation
To eliminate decrepitude
Study the absolute.

On Parting with the Buddhist Pilgrim Lingche

From the temple, deep in its tender bamboos,
Comes the low sound of an evening bell,
While the hat of a pilgrim carries the sunset
Farther and farther down the green mountain.

*Rejoicing that the Zen Master Bao Has Arrived from
Dragon Mountain*

What day did you come down from that former place,
spring grasses ready to turn green and fair?
Still it faces the mountain moon,
but who listens now to its rock-bound stream?
Monkey cries tell you night is fading;
blossoms that open show you the flowing years.
With metal staff you quietly come and go,
mindless—for everywhere is Zen.

A thousand clouds among a myriad streams
And in their midst a person at his ease.
By day he wanders through the dark green hills,
At night goes home to sleep beneath the cliffs.
Swiftly the changing seasons pass him by,
Tranquil, undefiled, no earthly ties.
Such pleasures!—and on what do they rely?
On a quiet calm, like autumn river water.

When men see Han-shan
They all say he's crazy
And not much to look at—
Dressed in rags and hides.
They don't get what I say
& I don't talk their language.
All I can say to those I meet:
"Try and make it to Cold Mountain."

HANSHAN
TR. GARY SNYDER

When the men of the world look for this path amid
     the clouds
It vanishes, with not a trace where it lay.
The high peaks have many precipices;
On the widest gulleys hardly a gleam falls.
Green walls close behind and before;
White clouds gather east and west.
Do you want to know where the cloud-path lies?
The cloud-path leads from sky to sky.

58   HANSHAN
     TR. ARTHUR WALEY

Men ask the way to Cold Mountain
Cold Mountain: there's no through trail.
In summer, ice doesn't melt
The rising sun blurs in swirling fog.
How did I make it?
My heart's not the same as yours.
If your heart was like mine
You'd get it and be right here.

Cold cliffs, more beautiful the deeper you enter—
Yet no one travels this road.
White clouds idle about the tall crags;
On the green peak a single monkey wails.
What other companions do I need?
I grow old doing as I please.
Though face and form alter with the years,
I hold fast to the pearl of the mind.

Clambering up the Cold Mountain path,
The Cold Mountain trail goes on and on:
The long gorge choked with scree and boulders,
The wide creek, the mist-blurred grass.
The moss is slippery, though there's been no rain
The pine sings, but there's no wind.
Who can leap the world's ties
And sit with me among the white clouds?

HANSHAN   61
TR. GARY SNYDER

As for me, I delight in the everyday Way,
Among mist-wrapped vines and rocky caves.
Here in the wilderness I am completely free,
With my friends, the white clouds, idling forever.
There are roads, but they do not reach the world;
Since I am mindless, who can rouse my thoughts?
On a bed of stone I sit, alone in the night,
While the round moon climbs up Cold Mountain.

So Han-shan writes you these words,
These words which no one will believe.
Honey is sweet; men love the taste.
Medicine is bitter and hard to swallow.
What soothes the feelings brings contentment,
What opposes the will calls forth anger.
Yet I ask you to look at the wooden puppets,
Worn out by their moment of play on stage!

A telling analogy for life and death:
Compare the two of them to water and ice.
Water draws together to become ice,
And ice disperses again to become water.
Whatever has died is sure to be born again;
Whatever is born comes round again to dying.
As ice and water do one another no harm,
So life and death, the two of them, are fine.

      TR. PETER HARRIS

In the third month when the silkworms were still small
The girls had time to go and gather flowers,
Along the wall they played with the butterflies,
Down by the water they pelted the old frog.
Into gauze sleeves they poured the ripe plums;
With their gold hairpins they dug up bamboo-sprouts.
With all that glitter of outward loveliness
How can the Cold Mountain hope to compete?

Why am I always so depressed?
Man's life is like the morning mushroom.
Who can bear, in a few dozen years,
To see new friends and old all gone away?
Thinking of this, I am filled with sadness,
A sadness I can hardly endure.
What shall I do? Say, what shall I do?
Take this old body home and hide it in the mountains!

TR. BURTON WATSON

Parrots dwell in the west country.
Foresters catch them with nets, to bring them to us.
Lovely women toy with them, morning and evening,
As they go to and from their courtyard pavilions.

They are given lordly gifts of golden cages—for their
    own storage!
Bolted in—their feathered coats are spoiled.
How unlike both swan and crane:
Wind-swirled and -tossed, they fly off into the clouds!

I sit and gaze on this highest peak of all;
Wherever I look there is distance without end.
I am all alone and no one knows I am here,
A lonely moon is mirrored in the cold pool.
Down in the pool there is not really a moon;
The only moon is in the sky above.
I sing to you this one piece of song;
But in the song there is not any Zen.

Yesterday I saw the trees by the river's edge,
Wrecked and broken beyond belief.
Only two or three trunks left standing,
Scarred by blades of a thousand axes.
Frost strips the yellowing leaves,
River waves pluck at withered roots.
This is the way the living must fare.
Why curse at Heaven and Earth?

Man, living in the dust,
Is like a bug trapped in a bowl.
All day he scrabbles round and round,
But never escapes from the bowl that holds him.
The immortals are beyond his reach,
His cravings have no end,
While months and years flow by like a river
Until, in an instant, he has grown old.

My mind is like the autumn moon
An emerald lake—pure, clean and bright.

There is nothing with which it compares;
Tell me, how can I explain?

HANSHAN
TR. ROBERT HENRICKS

You can see the moon's brightness,
Illuminating all under heaven.
Its round radiance, suspended in the Great Void,
Is lustrous, pure and ethereal.
Others say it waxes and wanes;
That which I see is eternal, never declining.
With an aura like the Mani pearl,
Its brilliance knows no day or night.

TR. JAMES HARGETT

Far, faraway, steep mountain paths,
Treacherous and narrow, ten thousand feet up;
Over boulders and bridges, lichens of green,
White clouds are often seen soaring,
A cascade suspends in mid-air like a bolt of silk;
The moon's reflection falls on a deep pool, glittering.
I shall climb up the magnificent mountain peak,
To await the arrival of a solitary crane.

I laugh at my failing strength in old age,
Yet still dote on pines and crags, to wander there in
  solitude.
How I regret that in all these past years until today,
I've let things run their course like an unanchored
  boat.

    TR. JAMES HARGETT

To what
Shall I compare the world?
    It is like the wake
Vanishing behind a boat
    that has rowed away at dawn.

Dhyana's Hall

At dawn I come to the convent old,
While the rising sun tips its tall trees with gold,—
As, darkly, by the winding path I reach
Dhyana's hall, hidden midst fir and beech.
Around these hills sweet birds their pleasure take,
Man's heart as free from shadow as this lake;
Here worldly sounds are hushed, as by a spell,
Save for the booming of the altar bell.

At Wang Changling's Retreat

Here, beside a clear deep lake,
You live accompanied by clouds;
Or soft through the pine the moon arrives
To be your own pure-hearted friend.
You rest under thatch in the shadow of your flowers,
Your dewy herbs flourish in their bed of moss.
Let me leave the world. Let me alight, like you,
On your western mountain with phoenixes and cranes.

Looking for Lu Hongjian but Failing to Find Him

You've moved to a house backing the outer wall;
I reach it by wild paths through mulberry and hemp.
Along the fence chrysanthemums newly set out
have yet to bloom, though autumn's here.
I pound the gate but no dog barks.
About to go, I ask at the house next door;
They tell me you're up in the hills,
never come home till the sun is low.

TR. BURTON WATSON

Idle Droning

Since earnestly studying the Buddhist doctrine of
    emptiness
I've learned to still all the common states of mind.
Only the devil of poetry I have yet to conquer—
let me come on a bit of scenery and I start my idle
    droning.

A Flower?

It seems a flower, but not a flower;
It seems a mist, but not a mist.
It comes at midnight,
It goes away in the morning.

Its coming is like a spring dream that does not last
    long,
And its going is like the morning cloud. You will find
    it nowhere.

    TR. CHING TI

Realizing the Futility of Life
[Written on the walls of a priest's cell, circa *828]*

Ever since the time when I was a lusty boy
Down till now when I am ill and old,
The things I have cared for have been different at
    different times,
But my being *busy*, that has never changed.
Then on the shore,—building sand-pagodas;
Now, at Court, covered with tinkling jade.
This and that,—equally childish games,
Things whose substance passes in a moment of time!
While the hands are busy, the heart cannot
    understand;
When there are no Scriptures, then Doctrine is sound.
Even should one zealously strive to learn the Way,
That very striving will make one's error more.

On his Baldness

At dawn I sighed to see my hairs fall;
At dusk I sighed to see my hairs fall.
For I dreaded the time when the last lock should go . . .
They are all gone and I do not mind at all!
I have done with that cumbrous washing and
      getting dry;
My tiresome comb for ever is laid aside.
Best of all, when the weather is hot and wet,
To have no top-knot weighing down on one's head!
I put aside my messy cloth wrap;
I have got rid of my dusty tasselled fringe.
In a silver jar I have stored a cold stream,
On my bald pate I trickle a ladle full.
Like one baptized with the Water of Buddha's Law,
I sit and receive this cool, cleansing joy.
Now I know why the priest who seeks Repose
Frees his heart by first shaving his head.

    TR. ARTHUR WALEY

Night Snow

I wondered why the covers felt so cold,
and then I saw how bright my window was.
Night far gone, I know the snow must be deep—
from time to time I hear the bamboos cracking.

The Temple

Autumn: the ninth year of Yuan Ho;
The eighth month, and the moon swelling her arc.
It was then I travelled to the Temple of Wu-chen,
A temple terraced on Wang Shun's Hill.
While still the mountain was many leagues away,
Of scurrying waters we heard the plash and fret.
From here the traveller, leaving carriage and horse,
Begins to wade through the shallows of the
    Blue Stream,
His hand pillared on a green holly-staff,
His feet treading the torrent's white stones.
A strange quiet stole on ears and eyes,
That knew no longer the blare of the human world.
From mountain-foot gazing at mountain-top,
Now we doubted if indeed it could be climbed;
Who had guessed that a path deep hidden there
Twisting and bending crept to the topmost brow?
Under the flagstaff we made our first halt;
Next we rested in the shadow of the Stone Shrine.
The shrine-room was scarce a cubit long,
With doors and windows unshuttered and unbarred.
I peered down, but could not see the dead;
Stalactites hung like a woman's hair.
Waked from sleep, a pair of white bats
Fled from the coffin with a whirr of snowy wings.

84

I turned away, and saw the Temple gate—
Scarlet eaves flanked by steeps of green;
'Twas as though a hand had ripped the mountain-side
And filled the cleft with a temple's walls and towers.
Within the gate, no level ground;
Little ground, but much empty sky.
Cells and cloisters, terraces and spires
High and low, followed the jut of the hill.
On rocky plateaux with no earth to hold
Were trees and shrubs, gnarled and very lean.
Roots and stems stretched to grip the stone;
Humped and bent, they writhed like a coiling snake.
In broken ranks pine and cassia stood,
Through the four seasons forever shady-green.
On tender twigs and delicate branches breathing
A quiet music played like strings in the wind.
Never pierced by the light of sun or moon,
Green locked with green, shade clasping shade.
A hidden bird sometimes softly sings;
Like a cricket's chirp sounds its muffled song.

At the Strangers' Arbour a while we stayed our steps;
We sat down, but had no mind to rest.
In a little while we had opened the northern door.
Ten thousand leagues suddenly stretched at our feet!
Brushing the eaves, shredded rainbows swept;
Circling the beams, clouds spun and whirled.

Through red sunlight white rain fell;
Azure and storm swam in a blended stream.
In a wild green clustered grasses and trees,
The eye's orbit swallowed the plain of Ch'in.
Wei River was too small to see;
The Mounds of Han, littler than a clenched fist.
I looked back; a line of red fence,
Broken and twisting, marked the way we had trod.
Far below, toiling one by one
Later climbers straggled on the face of the hill.

Straight before me were many Treasure Towers,
Whose wind-bells at the four corners sang.
At door and window, cornice and architrave
A thick cluster of gold and green-jade.
Some say that here the Buddha Kasyapa
Long ago quitted Life and Death.
Still they keep his iron begging-bowl,
With the furrow of his fingers chiselled deep at
        the base.
To the east there opens the jade Image Hall,
Where white Buddhas sit like serried trees.
We shook from our garments the journey's grime
        and dust,
And bowing worshipped those faces of frozen snow
Whose white cassocks like folded hoar-frost hung,
Whose beaded crowns glittered like a shower of hail.

We looked closer; surely Spirits willed
This handicraft, never chisel carved!
Next we climbed to the Chamber of Kuan-yin;
From afar we sniffed its odours of sandal-wood.
At the top of the steps each doffed his shoes;
With bated stride we crossed the Jasper Hall.
The Jewelled Mirror on six pillars propped,
The Four Seats cased in hammered gold
Through the black night glowed with beams of
      their own,
Nor had we need to light candle or lamp.
These many treasures in concert nodded and swayed—
Banners of coral, pendants of cornaline.
When the wind came jewels chimed and sang
Softly, softly like the music of Paradise.
White pearls like frozen dewdrops hanging;
Dark rubies spilt like clots of blood,
Spangled and sown on the Buddha's twisted hair,
Together fashioned his Sevenfold Jewel-crown.
In twin vases of pallid tourmaline
(Their colour colder than the waters of an autumn
      stream)
The calcined relics of Buddha's Body rest—
Rounded pebbles, smooth as the Specular Stone.
A jade flute, by angels long ago
Borne as a gift to the Garden of Jetavan!
It blows a music sweet as the crane's song

The Spirits of Heaven earthward well might draw.

It was at autumn's height,
The fifteenth day and the moon's orbit full.
Wide I flung the three eastern gates;
A golden spectra walked at the chapel-door!
And now with moonbeams jewel-beams strove,
In freshness and beauty darting a crystal light
That cooled the spirit and limbs of all it touched,
Nor night-long needed they to rest.
At dawn I sought the road to the Southern Tope,
Where wild bamboos nodded in clustered grace.
In the lonely forest no one crossed my path;
Beside me faltered a cold butterfly.
Mountain fruits whose names I did not know
With their prodigal bushes hedged the pathway in;
The hungry here copious food had found;
Idly I plucked, to test sour and sweet.

South of the road, the Spirit of the Blue Dell,
With his green umbrella and white paper pence!
When the year is closing, the people are ordered
        to grow,
As herbs of offering, marsil and motherwort;
So sacred the place, that never yet was stained
Its pure earth with sacrificial blood.

In a high cairn four or five rocks
Dangerously heaped, deep-scarred and heeling—
With what purpose did he that made the World
Pile them here at the eastern corner of the cliff!
Their slippery flank no foot has marked,
But mosses stipple like a flowered writing-scroll.
I came to the cairn, I climbed it right to the top;
Beneath my feet a measureless chasm dropped.
My eyes were dizzy, hand and knee quaked—
I did not dare bend my head and look.
A boisterous wind rose from under the rocks,
Seized me with it and tore the ground from my feet.
My shirt and robe fanned like mighty wings,
And wide-spreading bore me like a bird to the sky.
High about me, triangular and sharp,
Like a cluster of sword-points many summits rose.
The white mist that struck them in its airy course
They tore asunder, and carved a patch of blue.

And now the sun was sinking in the north-west;
His evening beams from a crimson globe he shed,
Till far beyond the great fields of green
His sulphurous disk suddenly down he drove.

And now the moon was rising in the south-east;
In waves of coolness the night air flowed.
From the grey bottom of the hundred-fathom pool

Shines out the image of the moon's golden disk!
Blue as its name, the Lan River flows
Singing and plashing forever day and night.
I gazed down; like a green finger-ring
In winding circuits it follows the curves of the hill,
Sometimes spreading to a wide, lazy stream,
Sometimes striding to a foamy cataract.
Out from the deepest and clearest pool of all,
In a strange froth the Dragon's-spittle flows.

I bent down; a dangerous ladder of stones
Paved beneath me a sheer and dizzy path.
I gripped the ivy, I walked on fallen trees,
Tracking the monkeys who came to drink at
        the stream.
Like a whirl of snowflakes the startled herons rose,
In damask dances the red sturgeon leapt.
For a while I rested, then plunging in the cool stream,
From my weary body I washed the stains away.
Deep or shallow, all was crystal clear;
I watched through the water my own thighs and feet.
Content I gazed at the stream's clear bed;
Wondered, but knew not, whence its waters flowed.

The eastern bank with rare stones is rife;
In serried courses the azure malachite,
That outward turns a smooth, glossy face;

In its deep core secret diamonds lie.
Pien of Ch'u died long ago,
And rare gems are often cast aside.
Sometimes a radiance leaks from the hill by night
To link its beams with the brightness of moon
and stars.

At the central dome, where the hills highest rise,
The sky is pillared on a column of green jade;
Where even the spotty lizard cannot climb
Can I, a man, foothold hope to find?
In the top is hollowed the White-lotus lake;
With purple cusps the clear waves are crowned.
The name I heard, but the place I could not reach;
Beyond the region of mortal things it lies.

And standing here, a flat rock I saw,
Cubit-square, like a great paving-stone,
Midway up fastened in the cliff-wall;
And down below it, a thousand-foot drop.
Here they say that a Master in ancient days
Sat till he conquered the concepts of Life and Death.
The place is called the Settled Heart Stone;
By aged men the tale is still told.

I turned back to the Shrine of Fairies' Tryst;
Thick creepers covered its old walls.

Here it was that a mortal long ago
On new-grown wings flew to the dark sky;
Westward a garden of agaric and rue
Faces the terrace where his magic herbs were dried.
And sometimes still on clear moonlit nights
In the sky is heard a yellow-crane's voice.

I turned and sought the Painted Dragon Hall,
Where the bearded figures of two ancient men
By the Holy Lectern at sermon-time are seen
In gleeful worship to nod their hoary heads;
Who, going home to their cave beneath the river,
Of weather-dragons the writhing shapes assume.
When rain is coming they puff a white smoke
In front of the steps, from a round hole in the stone.

Once a priest who copied the Holy Books
(of purpose dauntless and body undefiled)
Loved yonder pigeons, that far beyond the clouds
Fly in flocks beating a thousand wings.
They came and dropped him water in his writing-bowl;
Then sipped afresh in the river under the rocks.
Each day thrice they went and came,
Nor ever once missed their wonted time.
When the book was finished they sent for a holy priest,
A disciple of his, named Yang-nan.
He sang the hymns of the Lotus Blossom Book,

Again and again, a thousand, a million times.
His body perished, but his mouth still spoke,
The tongue resembling a red lotus-flower.
Today this relic is no longer shown;
But they still treasure the pyx in which it lies.

On a plastered wall are frescoes from the hand of Wu,
Whose pencil-colours never-fading glow.
On a white screen is writing by the master Ch'u,
The tones subtle as the day it first dried.

Magical prospects, monuments divine—
Now all were visited.
Here we had tarried five nights and days;
Yet homeward now with loitering footsteps trod.
I, that a man of the wild hills was born,
Floundering fell into the web of the World's net.
Caught in its trammels, they forced me to study books;
Twitched and tore me down the path of public life.
Soon I rose to be Bachelor of Arts;
In the Record Office, in the Censorate I sat.
My simple bluntness did not suit the times;
A profitless servant, I drew the royal pay.
The sense of this made me always ashamed,
And every pleasure a deep brooding dimmed.
To little purpose I sapped my heart's strength,
Till seeming age shrank my youthful frame.

From the very hour I doffed belt and cap
I marked how with them sorrow slank away.
But now that I wander in the freedom of streams
    and hills
My heart to its folly comfortably yields.
Like a wild deer that has torn the hunter's net
I range abroad by no halters barred.
Like a captive fish loosed into the Great Sea
To my marble basin I shall not ever return.
My body girt in the hermit's single dress,
My hand holding the Book of Chuang Chou,
On these hills at last I am come to dwell,
Loosed forever from the shackles of a trim world.
I have lived in labour forty years and more;
If Life's remnant vacantly I spend,
Seventy being our span, then thirty years
Of idleness are still left to live.

At Yiye Temple

I play with stones and sit beside the stream,
I search for flowers and walk around the temple.
Sometimes I listen to the songs of birds;
The sounds of spring are everywhere.

Meditation Hall

Clear the land, thatch the rush for roof,
all around cherish the empty, the pure.
Mountain blossoms fall by a secluded door,
within, one who has forgotten the world's schemings.
Concern with existence needs no possession,
comprehending the void does not wait upon reason.
All things are of conditions born,
profound is the silence in the midst of clamor.
A man's mind is very much the same;
A bird in flight, leaving no tracks behind.

An Early Morning Visit to the Buddhist Priest Chao to
Read the Chan Scriptures

Drawing water from the well,
   I rinse my cold teeth,
I brush the dust from my clothes
   and purify my mind;
Calmly I turn the leaves of a Buddhist sutra
And recite as I stroll out of the east study.

The true Way has not been accepted—
False tracks are what the world follows.
Buddha's teaching promises joy after Nirvana:
How can I master with it my habitual nature?

Here in the quiet of the priest's courtyard,
The green of the moss blends with the dense bamboos;
As the sun breaks through the strands of damp mist
It bathes the blue pines as if with oil.

Such freshness!—hard to express in words . . .
Enlightened, satisfied,
   my heart is at peace.

Looking for the Recluse and Not Finding Him Home

I asked his servant under the pines,
he said: "The master has gone to pick herbs.
He is somewhere out there in the hills,
But the clouds are so deep I know not where."

Southern Study

Alone I lie in the southern study,
My soul at ease; the scene is also bare.
There is a mountain which comes onto my pillow,
But no troubles get into my mind.
The blind rolls up the moon that hits the bed;
Screens block the wind from entering the room.
I wait for spring—spring hasn't arrived yet—
It ought to be east of the sea-gates.

To an Old Monk on Mount Tian Tai

Living alone where none other dwells,
shrine among the pines where mountain tints
    encroach,
old man's been ninety years a monk:
heart beyond the clouds a lifetime long.
White hair hangs down, his head's unshaven:
clear black pupils smile deep mysteries.
He can still point to the orphan moon
for me alone, relaxes his discipline, this moment.

Written on Master Hengzhao's Wall

A Zen path
The autumn moss grows over;
Icy windows bear streaks
Of rain.

The true mind
mysteriously integrates
Itself, but who appreciates
Good poems? Dew chills;
Cricket noises muffle.
A light wind fans
Shadows of foliage.

As if intent,
All day in the window
White clouds.

Grieving for Zen Master Jianzhang

A frosty bell
Anxiously overrides the waterclock;
Grieving together,
Dense sorrow dawns.

Guests from the coast
Exchange his enlightened poems;
Monks from these woods
Describe his bearing while ill.
The cleansing spring
Floats a fallen leaf;
On rock concentrations
Chirping crickets assemble.

Turning, I view
Cloud Gate Mountain:
Dwindling Sun descends
The distant peak.

TR. PAUL HANSEN

On the Winter Festival I Visited Lone Mountain
and the Two Monks Huijin and Huisi

The sky looked like snow,
   clouds were filling the lake,
terrace and tower appeared and vanished,
   the hills seemed there, then gone.

Waters so clear that stones were revealed,
   and I could count the fish;
deep in the woods there was no one,
   birds called each to the other.

On this winter festival I didn't go home
   to be with children and wife,
I sought these holy men, known by repute,
   which was really to please myself.

Where was the holy men's lodging found?—
in front of Jewel Cloud Mountain
   where the road twists and turns.

There was Lone Mountain, so completely alone
   who would build his hut here?—
yet if holy men have the holy Way
   then the mountain cannot be lonely.

Paper windows and bamboo roof,
    deep within it was warm,
wrapped in cassocks they sat asleep
    on mats for meditation.

The cold weather and journey's distance
    made my servant worried;
the carriage was readied, I hurried back,
    before it was late afternoon.

When we left the mountain I turned to gaze—
    it was covered by clouds and trees,
and all I could see was a wild hawk
    circling the pagoda.

The very blandness of this trip
    left its residue of pleasure:
When I reached home I was in a daze,
    still shaking myself from dream.

I wrote this poem as swift as fire
    to catch what was fleeting away,
For once a clear scene escapes us
    it cannot be grasped again.

Written on Abbot Lun's Wall at Mount Jiao

The dharma master lives here at Mount Chiao,
And yet, in fact, has never lived here at all.
I've come here to ask about the dharma,
But the dharma master sees through me and
     says nothing.
It isn't that the dharma master lacks the words,
But that I do not understand the nature of his reply.
Look, sir, at how your head and your feet
Are capped and shod without a second thought.
It is like the man who had a long beard,
But did not anguish at its length
Until one day someone asked him
How he arranged it when he went to bed.
Then he put it inside then outside the coverlet,
The whole night spent looking for the best position.
So he tossed and turned until the dawn of day,
And in the end wanted only to chop it off!
Although this fable is light and humorous,
Still it contains a much deeper meaning.
When I asked the dharma master about this,
He gave a smile and nodded in assent.

SU DONGPO
TR. BEATA GRANT

[*According to Dogen, Master Changcong was once asked by a monk, "Do inanimate objects preach the Law?", to which he replied, "Continuously." Su Dongpo spent an entire night wrestling with this koan and at dawn wrote this poem.*]

The murmuring brook is the Buddha's long, broad
      tongue.
And is not the shapely mountain the body of purity?
Through the night I listen to eighty thousand *gathas*,
When dawn breaks, how will I explain it to others?

The Lyre

Some say music lurks in the lyre;
Why, then, closed in its case is it dumb?
Some say the sound comes from the fingers of
    the player;
Why then on yours do we hear none?

SU DONGPO

TR. YANG XIANYI AND GLADYS YANG

Flower Shadows

In rows and heaps
The blossoms crowd
Upon the jade-green terrace.
Several times have I summoned my boy
To sweep them away.
His efforts have had but small success,
For no sooner does the sunset
Carry them off
Than the bright moon,
Rising,
Gathers and brings them again.

    TR. HENRY HART

Spring Night

The few minutes of a Spring night
Are worth ten thousand pieces of gold.
The perfume of the flowers is so pure.
The shadows of the moon are so black.
In the pavilion the voices and flutes are so high
      and light.
In the garden a hammock rocks
In the night so deep, so profound.

Days of Rain; the Rivers Have Overflowed

Drenching rain hisses down, cooling the evening;
I lie and listen to banyan noise echo on the porch.
By feeble lamp shine, I shake off a dream;
curtains and blinds, half soaked, breathe old incense.
High waves shake the bed, spray blows from
     the cistern;
dark wind rocks the trees—they clink like jade.
Even if it clears I have no place to go—
let it keep on all night pelting the empty stairs.

Begonias

The East wind blows gently.
The rising rays float
On the thick perfumed mist.
The moon appears, right there,
At the corner of the balcony.
I only fear in the depth of night
The flowers will fall asleep.
I hold up a gilded candle
To shine on their scarlet beauty.

SU DONGPO

TR. KENNETH REXROTH

Passing Over Dayu Peak

In a moment, all my defilements have vanished,
Leaving both body and soul transparently pure.
So vast is it here between heaven and earth
That even alone, all is well with me.
Today as I travel along the mountain peaks
Self and world are once and for all forgotten.
The winds of the immortals seem to caress my head,
As, tying up my hair, I receive their secrets.

The Southern Room over the River

The room is prepared, the incense burned.
I close the shutters before I close my eyelids.
The patterns of the quilt repeat the waves of the river.
The gauze curtain is like a mist.
Then a dream comes to me and when I awake
I no longer know where I am.
I open the western window and watch the waves
Stretching on and on to the horizon.

SU DONGPO
TR. KENNETH REXROTH

Recalling the Old Days at Mianchi

To what can we liken human life?
Perhaps to a wild swan's footprints on mud or snow;
By chance its claws imprint the mud
Before it flies off at random, east or west.
The old monk is dead and a new pagoda built;
The old wall has crumbled, the poem we wrote on
    it gone.
Do you still remember this rugged mountain path,
The long way, our exhaustion and how the lame
    donkey brayed?

    TR. YANG XIANYI AND GLADYS YANG

Moving to Lin'gao Pavilion

We are born between heaven and earth,
Solitary ants riding a huge millstone.
For all our paltry attempts to move to the right,
We are helplessly turned by the wind wheel to the left.
Although I have practised benevolence and
      righteousness,
I have still not been able to escape hunger and cold.
The sword-blade pot—a perilous way to cook rice!
The spiked mat—no restful sitting there.
But do I not have these lovely mountains and streams?
Besides, in a blink of an eye, the storm will have passed,
Although one need not wait until old age to retire,
How many men have had the courage not to?
I am lucky to have been put out to pasture,
Like a weary horse that has had its load removed.
My family has the run of this river post house.
At the tunnel's end, Heaven poked a finger through
      for me:
These good things balance out the hunger and poverty.
I have no need for either condolences or
      congratulations!
Tranquil and calm, I feel neither joy nor sorrow,
And so won't turn these words about hardship into
      a song.

SU DONGPO
TR. BEATA GRANT

Enjoying the Peonies at the Temple of Good Fortune

In my old age I adorn myself with flowers, blush not;
It is the flowers that should blush for decking an old
    man's head.
Half tipsy I fumble along home, and men must be
    laughing at me,
For along the road half the folk have hooked up
    their blinds.

    TR. ROBERT KOTEWALL AND NORMAN SMITH

Presented to Tanxiu

He is like white clouds rising from the mountains—
No-mind from the start,
He is like the roosting bird who feels no longing
For the woods of home.
But because this man of the Way happens to enjoy
The mountains and streams
He wanders among them unconcerned about how deep
Into the lakeside mountain peaks he goes.
He has gone to the empty cliffs to worship
The hundred thousand forms of the Buddha,
And now wishes to visit Ts'ao-hsi and pay his respects
To the relics of the Sixth Patriarch.
If you want to know whether the water is hot or cold,
You must taste it for yourself.
I am beginning to think the dream I had of you
Was not an illusion after all!
In that dream you suddenly pulled from your sleeve
A sutra written on papyrus leaves,
Its lines and phrases jade-pure as the moon,
And stars strung together like pearls.
There are many beautiful spots in this world,
And he has just about seen them all:
From the southern peaks of Mount Lu
All the way to West Lake—
West Lake, which, if one looks to the north,

Lies three thousand *li* away,
Its great dike stretching out unbroken
Across the autumn waters.
As I chant the verses the master wrote
Describing the beauty of Mount Nan-p'ing,
The miasmic summer airs of Hui-chou
Seem to vanish in an autumn breeze.
Is it possible that the pleasure of your company
Will end in but ten short days?
Cutting through the brambles, it won't be easy
To find the road home again.
The wild greens I use to entice the master to stay
Are not much to speak of:
Oh how I look forward to the season
When the lichees turn red.

The Weaker the Wine

> *"The weakest wine is better than warm water.*
> *Rags are better than no clothes at all.*
> *An ugly wife and a quarrelsome concubine*
> *Are better than an empty house."*

The weaker the wine,
The easier it is to drink two cups.
The thinner the robe,
The easier it is to wear it double.
Ugliness and beauty are opposites,
But when you're drunk, one is as good as the other.
Ugly wives and quarrelsome concubines,
The older they grow, the more they're alike.
Live unknown if you would realize your end.
Follow the advice of your common sense.
Avoid the Imperial Audience
Chamber, the Eastern Flowery Hall.
The dust of the times and the wind of the
       Northern Pass.
One hundred years is a long time,
But at last it comes to an end.
Meanwhile it is no greater accomplishment
To be a rich corpse or a poor one.
Jewels of jade and pearl are put in the mouths
Of the illustrious dead

To conserve their bodies.
They do them no good, but after a thousand years,
They feed the robbers of their tombs.
As for literature, it is its own reward.
Fortunately fools pay little attention to it.
A chance for graft makes them blush with joy.
Good men are their own worst enemies.
Wine is the best reward of merit.
In all the world, good and evil,
Joy and sorrow, are in fact
Only aspects of the void.

TR. KENNETH REXROTH

Sending Off Chan Master Xiaoben to Fayun

As long as one dwells beneath this heavenly roof,
No matter where one goes there will be dues to pay.
Even if one lives peacefully with no business affairs,
How can one pass one's life without trouble of
     some kind!
In mountain groves too there is worry and pain—
Even official robes and carriages are part of the play.
I have not yet been able to retire to the quiet life,
But you, Master, should be living in peaceful seclusion!
The Imperial City is full of brilliant scholars,
Discussing, debating, distinguishing black from white.
Asked to name the first principle of Divine Truth,
Bodhidharma faced the emperor and said,
    "Who knows?"
Master, what business brings you to this place,
Like a solitary moon suspended in the empty blue?
When was this self that is like a floating cloud,
Ever limited by the boundaries of north and south?
If one leaves one's mountain having achieved no-mind,
Then when it rains, one will still be able to find refuge.
Long ago I made a promise to you by the Pearl Stream,
When will I return there to hang up my flask
    and staff?

SU DONGPO
TR. BEATA GRANT

Abbot Zhan's Cell

He sounds the evening drum himself, the early
     morning bell;
His door closes on a single pillow, a flickering lamp;
After poking the red embers among white ashes
He lies down to hear the patter of rain on his window.

TR. YANG XIANYI AND GLADYS YANG

Written on the Wall at Xilin Temple

Regarded from one side, an entire range;
    from another, a single peak.
Far, near, high, low, all its parts
    different from the others.
If the true face of Mount Lu
    cannot be known,
It is because the one looking at it
    is standing in its midst.

SU DONGPO   123
TR. BEATA GRANT

Books

It is when we are near the end of a book that we
     enjoy it.
Guests whom we anxiously expect often fail to come.
So the world runs always contrary to our wishes.
How rarely in a hundred years do we open our hearts!

Every single thing
Changes and is changing
Always in this world.
Yet with the same light
The moon goes on shining.

SAIGYO

TR. GEOFFREY BOWNAS AND ANTHONY
THWAITE

The winds of spring
Scattered the flowers
As I dreamt my dream.
Now I awaken,
My heart is disturbed.

TR. GEOFFREY BOWNAS AND ANTHONY
THWAITE

Trailing on the wind,
The smoke from Mount Fuji
Melts into the sky.
So too my thoughts—
Unknown their resting place.

SAIGYO
TR. GEOFFREY BOWNAS AND ANTHONY
THWAITE

To "Eyes' fascination"

Mellow, mellow at the sun's foot floats the purple mist;
The genial warmth dismisses my light fur.
Tired by the breath of heaven,
Drunk with the breath of flowers,
I dream at noontide with head on hands.

This lazy Spring is like the water of a pond in
     Springtime—
Wrinkled as by sorrow like a strip of crape.
Gently, gently, dragging and dragging,
The East Wind, strengthless,
Tries to make a ripple, but gives up.

TR. ROBERT KOTEWALL AND NORMAN SMITH

The Boatman's Flute

Today there is no wind on the Yangtze;
the water is calm and green
with no waves or ripples.
All around the boat
light floats in the air
over a thousand acres of smooth, lustrous jade.

One of the boatmen wants to break the silence.
High on wine, he picks up his flute
and plays into the mist.
The clear music rises to the sky—
    an ape in the mountains
    screaming at the moon;
    a creek rushing through a gully.
Someone accompanies on the sheepskin drum,
    his head held steady as a peak,
    his fingers beating like raindrops.

A fish breaks the crystal surface of the water
and leaps ten feet into the air.

YANG WANLI
TR. JONATHAN CHAVES

Making Fire in the Boat on a Snowy Day

Raven silver charcoal catches fire and gives forth
    green fog,
So I pretend it's a large stick of heavy aloes incense.
Stopping, then starting, it billows forth thickly;
Scattered into a fine mist, it warms my robe and
    trousers.
But in a moment the fog clears, spitting out red rays,
And blazes like the rising sun on cloud surfaces.
This bright spring, mild sun warm my whole room;
My pale face reddens; I think I'm in the Land
    of Drunks!
Suddenly the fire grows cold, and the fog all
    disappears;
All I see is snowy ash piled up in my red stove.
Outside my window the snow is more than three
    feet deep,
But this snow inside my window is only one inch
    fragrant!

Red Peonies in a Jar

Afraid that the autumn wind
   might be jealous of the peonies,
I cut a branch and put it
   in a porcelain vase.
The heavy curtains are drawn,
   the doors are closed—
why do the petals keep falling off?

The Cold Lantern

Old and young, everyone's asleep.
The cold lantern, flickering at midnight,
    is my only companion.
The two flowers I've been looking at become
        dragonfly eyes;
the single flame, a jade vase hanging in the air.

        TR. JONATHAN CHAVES

Passing the Pavilion on Shenzhu Bridge

I get down from my palanquin
    and look around the country inn.
I'm surprised by the cold sound of water beneath
      my feet.
The Yangtze River is closer than I thought:
suddenly, above the bamboo grove,
    an inch of mast floats by.

YANG WANLI
TR. JONATHAN CHAVES

Spending the Night at the River-Port Pool Rock

At the third watch, no moon, the sky's really black;
A flash of lightning is followed by the roar of thunder.
Rain pierces the sky, falling on my boat-hut's roof;
A driving wind blows across, crooked, then straight.
The loose matting leaks, soaking my bedding;
The sound of waves beats my pillow, a paper's
    width away.
In the middle of dreams, I am startled awake and
    can't sleep.
Grabbing my clothes, I sit up straight and sigh over
    and over.
I have experienced every difficulty and hardship during
    my travels,
But in my whole life there's been nothing like tonight!
Lord Heaven scares me with his nasty jokes;
Without informing me, he gave me this surprise.
He may not be able to suddenly gather his wind or tidy
    his rain;
Yet can I now ask him for the east to get light?
I hang my head, draw in my legs, how narrow and
    confined!
When suddenly once more, on my head—drrippp!!!

    TR. J. D. SCHMIDT

Rising Early

Chrysanthemums in bloom—as gaunt as ever;
peonies, leaves falling off, seem completely withered.
A locust, frozen nearly to death,
clings desperately to a cold branch.

The Morning Ferry

Through the mist
The river and the mountains are dimly seen,
And from the crowing of the roosters
And the barking of the dogs
I would surmise that we are passing a village.
The little ferry has a coat of thick frost;
And when I set my foot upon a board,
My shoe leaves its perfect print upon it.

136   YANG WANLI
      TR. HENRY HART

Staying Overnight at Xiaosha Stream

Trees, laced in mountain mist,
    patch broken clouds;
the wind scatters a rainstorm of fragrant petals.
The green willows, it is said, are without feeling—
why then do they try so hard to touch the traveller
    with their catkins?

YANG WANLI   137
TR. JONATHAN CHAVES

During an Intercalary August After The "Arrival of Autumn" It Was Hot in the Evening and I Went to Be Cool in the Prefectural Garden

When I made it to the top of the wall,
    at once my eyes saw clearly:
twilight hills were rivals to offer me
    several sharp points of green.
Then weeping willows ceased their dance
    of leaves within west wind—
for the longest time one leaf alone
    did not stop.

The Twin Pagodas of Orchid Stream

The tall pagoda is not pointed, the short one is.
One of them wears an embroidered robe,
   the other a silver skirt.
Do you wonder why they never say a word?
It's because the rapids speak for them
   with the voice of Buddha.

Don't Read Books!

Don't read books!
Don't chant poems!
When you read books your eyeballs wither away,
    leaving the bare sockets.
When you chant poems your heart leaks out slowly
    with each word.
People say reading books is enjoyable.
People say chanting poems is fun.
But if your lips constantly make a sound
    like an insect chirping in autumn,
you will only turn into a haggard old man.
And even if you don't turn into a haggard old man,
it's annoying for others to have to hear you.

It's so much better
    to close your eyes, sit in your study,
    lower the curtains, sweep the floor,
    burn incense.
It's beautiful to listen to the wind,
    listen to the rain,
take a walk when you feel energetic,
and when you're tired go to sleep.

On Seeing the First Bloom of the Lotus

Here it is: this
   must be that spring to come,
outside the vexing world:
   lotus blossoms opening
through my door, in the dawn sky.

JAKUREN   141
TR. STEVEN CARTER

Watching the Moon Go Down

Set now,
and I too will go below
the rim of the hill—
so night after night
let us keep company

Bright bright!
bright bright bright!
bright bright!
bright bright bright!
bright bright, the moon!

Coming, going, the waterfowl
Leaves not a trace,
Nor does it need a guide.

TR. LUCIEN STRYK AND TAKASHI IKEMOTO

Depending on Neither Words nor Letters

Since it is no part
   of the words we toss aside
   so casually
it leaves no trace of itself
   in the marks of the brush.

Worship Service

In a snowfall
   that obscures the winter grasses
a white heron—
using his own form
   to hide himself away.

Impromptu Poem [no. 9 of a series]

The sky over the bay ahead a mass of cloud,
Now dark, now light, reflecting the setting sun's rays,
Back feathers light black, belly feathers white—
I watch the flock of sea birds turn and wheel in flight.

KOKAN SHIREN
TR. DAVID POLLACK

Winter Moon

A mountain grove, leafless—
Cloudless skies, windstill—
Dawn colors pinch the frost; chill moonlight overflows;
All heaven and earth should bear the name-board
    "Palace of Broad Cold."

Winter Moon (2)

Opening the window at midnight, the night air cold,
Garden and roof a gleaming white,
I go to the verandah, stretch out my hand to scoop up
        some snow—
Didn't I know that moonlight won't make a ball?

Summer Night

To escape the heat I sleep upstairs
Where a slight cool grows in the night:
A frog's croak echoes in a stone basin,
Moonlight casts patterns through bamboo blinds;
I accept every sound and sight that's offered,
The more detached, the more I hear and see;
A time of night I am so truly still
I no longer notice the mosquitos buzzing round
     my ears.

Refreshing, the wind against the waterfall
As the moon hangs, a lantern, on the peak
And the bamboo window glows. In old age mountains
Are more beautiful than ever. My resolve:
That these bones be purified by rocks.

JAKUSHITSU GENKO   151
TR. LUCIEN STRYK AND TAKASHI IKEMOTO

Cold Night: Impromptu

Wind stirs the cold woods, a frosty moon gleams,
Absorbed in talk of elevated things, midnight come and
      gone,
(Roast yams on skewers lie forgotten in the hearth)
Silently we listen to the sound of leaves raining on the
      window.

Autumn's Whiteness

Autumn gales drive the shimmering silver saucer of
    the moon;
Its reflection falls on the clear river, cold as a great
    length of glossy silk.
Even if red flowers of waterwort were added to these
    banks
For the man of the Way there is only perception of the
    one-color realm.

SESSON YUBAI
TR. MARIAN URY

*[Written in China when imprisoned by the Mongols and
facing possible death]*

In heaven and earth, no ground to plant my
    single staff,
but I can hide this body where no trace will be found.
At midnight the wooden man mounts his horse of
    stone,
crashing through a hundred, a thousand folds
    of encircling iron.

I delight that man is nothing, all things nothing,
a thousand worlds complete in my one cage.
Blame forgotten, mind demolished, a three-Zen joy—
who says Devadatta is in hell?

Wonderful, this three-foot sword of the Great Yüan,
sparkling with cold frost over ten thousand miles.
Though the skull goes dry, these eyes will see again.
My white gem worth a string of cities has never had
    a flaw.

Like lightning it flashes through the shadows, severing
    the spring wind.
The god of nothingness bleeds crimson, streaming,
Mount Sumeru to my amazement turns upside down.
I will dive, disappear into the stem of the lotus.

154   SESSON YUBAI
     TR. BURTON WATSON

*Staying at Luyuan Temple: Wang Wei's Former
Residence*

Dilapidated and deserted, this Tang Dynasty temple,
The man who once lived here long since gone;
Over mountains folded like a thousand layers of silk,
A few sunset rays still linger in a transitory world.
Pagodas loom up out of mountain mists,
Bell sounds choke in the blowing wind . . .
Gazing from my window I put a halt to such regrets:
At the graveyard gate I'll meet him coming back.

SESSON YUBAI   155
TR. DAVID POLLACK

Miscellaneous Poems from My Lair

1

Old rat as usual stealing oil from my lamp,
With squeaking screeches leaps about, poking holes
    in the walls;
And I as usual grab the broom and hurl it through
    the dark—
If I ever hit him they can put down one more rat-soul
    for the Western Heaven!

2

Dream of rivers and lakes broken, I sit at midnight in
    the meditation hall;
From empty steps come the steady sounds of long
    summer rains:
Blink, blonk—the temple roof leaks everywhere,
And every drop stabs clear into my guts.

3

By now I'd be the old dragon rock of Mount Lu,
White-bearded, grizzle-haired, stern-visaged—
But the temple gate wasn't firmly locked,
And someone's come to pass the time chitchatting . . .

4

Yakkety-yak: "The textbook's inane, can't you
    see that?
Stupid business, this facing a wall—I'm worn out from
    the effort."
I make a deep basket of my sleeves, keep my tongue
    to myself—
When I open *my* mouth it'll be at mealtime!

5

A myriad trees sway in the wind, yellow leaves
    flutter down;
The cold color of mountains all around, I don't
    open my gate:
Someone once planted these cedars in the garden
Just to keep half a day's sunshine from these
    thatched eaves.

Rhyming with the Priest Caoan's Poem "Living in the Mountains" [no. 7 of a series]

Cranes in the wilderness, lonely clouds—their
    destination is uncertain:
Where in this world am I to address my deepest
    thoughts?
Forest trees in serried ranks ascend the cliff walls,
Like a series of brush strokes, hills and peaks arrayed
    out to the horizon;
My mind brims with Zen clear as water,
Old bones jut angularly thin as kindling;
Fame is nothing one can keep for long—
A hundred years of light and dark before we reach
    the end.

In the Mountain

Yellow chrysanthemums and green bamboo,
    they don't belong to others.
Bright moon and clear breeze
    are not for the sphere of the senses.
They're all treasures
    of my house—
Fetch them home freely
    use them, get to know them!

At Tomo Harbor

Cold wind in the southern trees: autumn in the city
    by the sea;
The smoke of war-fires vanished but the ashes not
    yet cleared away—
Singing girls, knowing nothing of the destruction
    of the state,
Clamor-and-clang forth their tunes as they sail
    upon orchid boats.

Imitating the Old Style

Strong, strong is the wind of the Last Days;
from the earth dust rises, swirl upon swirl.
In the heavens, the sun shines faintly;
in the world of men, both good and evil flourish.
Mole crickets and ants go after stench and filth;
but the phoenix perches on the parasol tree.
Here there is one man far from worldly concerns:
he moves freely among the white clouds.

In China: Sick with Malarial Fever

Every nasty bug has schemed to plague me with
 disease,
The twin Gods of Illness bore holes in my chest
 and diaphragm
("He's old—why not kill him off?"),
Send vermin of darkness to release their poisonous
 venom.

The suffocating heat of my body has steamed my
 vitality away,
I quake as though struck by thunder;
Heaven and earth have become a gigantic two-part
 steamer
And all the gravy pours out of me.
But suddenly comes a chill to chase away the heat,
And I shiver as though drowning under ice,
Pile up more blankets over coverlets and quilts,
No end to the number I can take.

Why, in such a brief span of time,
Do Yin and Yang alternate so violently?
I cough and I sneeze,
Tears running mixed with phlegm,
Toss and turn but can't find peace
No matter how I rearrange pillow and mattress;

I have trouble whether I'm up or down,
For the slightest movement someone must support me,
So dizzy I confuse square and round,
Fall over all the time, go black and blank out.

All my life I've eaten a vegetarian diet,
And it's always suited my taste just fine:
So the five whole mullet they've set before me now
Taste about as appetizing as frozen quinine bark.
In the short while I've been confined to this hammock,
My scrawny body has turned to jerky;
People passing by look in
Wondering if I'm not dead and just pretending to
    be alive.

All day groans issue from my mouth—
Whatever comes brings anger or terror.
Returning to consciousness, I compose myself:
A visitor from far across the seas,
No one knows my mind
Or has pity for a strange accent.

CHUGAN ENGETSU   163
TR. DAVID POLLACK

Herding the Ox in the Himalayas

Chew the glossy, tender leaves—
You'll know the sweet and the sour.
Snow lies thick in the hottest summer,
Spring lingers in the coldest winter.
You wish to lean, then lean;
You wish to lie down, then lie down.
Seeing this, Shih-te roars with laughter,
And Han-shan opens his mouth wide.

TR. PETER LEE

At Deathbed

Life is like a bubble—
Some eighty years, a spring dream.
Now I'll throw away this leather sack,
A crimson sun sinks on the west peak!

To Rhyme with a Poem by My Old Teacher:
Sick in Winter

Driven against the paper windows, flying sleet borne
　　on a sour wind;
Sitting on a mat, hanging lamp left unlit, I watch the
　　desolate scene.
The sound of a dark brown hungry rat overturning
　　a stoneware jar
Strikes my ears like the knelling of a bell.

For all these years, my certain Zen:
Neither I nor the world exist.
The sutras neat within the box,
My cane hooked upon the wall,
I lie at peace in moonlight
Or, hearing water plashing on the rock,
Sit up: none can purchase pleasure such as this:
Spangled across the step-moss, a million coins!

Sweeping Leaves

Lacking cash to buy firewood,
I sweep up leaves from the road in front,
Each one as valuable as gold;
Piled up like gorgeous red brocades,
I covet them greedily for warming my knees
And to bring some comfort to my cold heart:
I'll take them back to burn in the hearth while I sit
    in meditation,
And return to listening to the rain dripping on
    the steps.

In the Mountains

With the true emptiness of nonaction,
I nap on a stone pillow among rocks.
Do you ask me what is my power?
A single tattered robe through life!

Inscription over his Door

He who holds that nothingness
Is formless, flowers are visions,
Let him enter boldly!

TR. LUCIEN STRYK AND TAKASHI IKEMOTO

Camellia Blossoms

My ancient hut's a ruin, half-hidden under moss—
Who'd have his carriage pause before my gate?
But my servant boy understands that I've beckoned
    an honoured guest
For he leaves unswept the camellia blossoms that
    fill the ground.

Hymn for Offering Incense Upon the Buddha's Attainment of the Path

The morning star returns night after night
The snows of the twelfth month linger from year
      to year
Silly:
    Gautama's achieving some "special" state;
Looking for a knife in the water by marks in the
      ship's hull

Inscribed on the Pavilion of Moon on the Water:
Two Poems

1
In the water is a moon gleaming like gold
That I greedily watch at my open window deep into
      each night;
My sick eyes suddenly cause another to appear—
A monkey's leaped into the blue ripples of my mind!

2
By the light of the moon in the water I sit in
      meditation,
A wide Palace of Cold soaking into smooth, blue grass;
At midnight I rise, turn suddenly around,
And find the perfect circle of moon in the heart of
      the ripples.

GIDO SHUSHIN

TR. DAVID POLLACK

Improvisation Upon Leaving the Nanzenji to Go Into Retirement

Vast sea of pain; waves cling to the sky!
Eight winds of passion drive my leaking boat.
Though I've others yet to rescue I'll first pole for the
    nearer shore
To drift as of old in the shallows, by the banks among
    flowering reeds.

Poem Rhyming with the Monk San's "Trip to Kanazawa—Recalling Old Times"

Miserably cold, the temple before dawn,
Still and lonely, few monks to be seen;
The temple is old, with soot-blackened walls,
The pond overgrown, its surface like folds in a robe;
Incense before the Buddha has burned, gone out,
    turned cold,
The sermon over, blossoms fly in the rain;
I've reached the point of doing away with happiness
    and sadness—
A white board door swinging to and fro in the breeze.

GIDO SHUSHIN   175
TR. DAVID POLLACK

Rohatsu: To Show to My Disciples

[Rohatsu, the eighth day of the twelfth month, was thought to be the day the Buddha (sometimes called "the curly-headed fellow") achieved enlightenment.]

The older one gets, the harder it is to achieve
    Buddhahood;
Ill now, I'm too weary to leave the temple.
But for the rest of you who must make it across,
The ways of the world are more difficult still.
I wake, stars hang low over the doorway,
The sky lightens, snow hugs the gate;
I feel sympathy for that old curly-headed fellow,
Barefoot, descending his long, steep slope.

Two Scenes Inscribed on a Screen

1

Somewhere, a fishing boat arranges its lines—
Evening brings wind and rain, fishing's been slow;
From the houses on the shore on the other side of the
     willow trees,
A tavern flag gleams in the thicket of kitchen-smoke.

2

Evening snow hurries them homeward; the road
     twists, the going slow—
But why isn't the master riding on his donkey?
It walks alone, led by a country lad
To help it across the bridges over the gorges—no fear
     of danger.

GIDO SHUSHIN
TR. DAVID POLLACK

In Response to a Request to "Explain the Secret Teaching"

If I explained aloud, then it wouldn't be a true
    explanation,
And if I transmitted it on paper, then where would be
    the secret?
At a western window on a rainy autumn night,
White hair in the guttering lamplight, asleep facing
    the bed . . .

The Painted Fan

Dim fringe of cloud and lustrous moon-disc:
The little boats have left for harbor; now is dusk.
Surely the fishers need not fear that their homes may
    be hard to find:
Village under plum blossoms radiant at river's edge.

An Old Temple

Which way did it face? this ancient temple gate,
Wisteria vines deep on all four walls.
Flowers near the eaves lie crushed after the rains;
Wild birds sing for the visitor alone.
Grass engulfs the seat of the World-Honored One,
And from its base has melted the patron's gold.
These broken tablets show no years or months—
Hard to tell whether they're from T'ang or Sung.

The void has collapsed upon the earth,
Stars, burning, shoot across Iron Mountain.
Turning a somersault, I brush past.

Dwelling in the Mountains:
A Poem Rhyming with Chanyue's [no. 5 in a series]

Few people know of this nest hidden in an
     out-of-the-way spot,
Where the dark green of ivy on ancient trees
     gleams in the doorway.
Their meal of sweet-smelling grasses over,
     grey deer sleep;
Having picked all the small pears, white monkeys
     have scattered.
Washing my robe in creek water, I trouble
     the clouds' reflections,
Delight in the play of the sunlight on herbs
     drying from sunny eaves;
The servant lad, unable to comprehend the notion
     of "permanence in change,"
Reproaches me each morning with the thinness
     of my hair.

     TR. DAVID POLLACK

Like dew that vanishes,
like a phantom that disappears,
or the light cast
    by a flash of lightning—
so should one think of oneself.

IKKYU SOJUN
TR. STEVEN CARTER

Contemplating the Law, reading sutras, trying to be a
    real master;
yellow robes, the stick, the shouts, till my wooden
    seat's all crooked;
but it seems my real business was always in the muck,
with my great passion for women, and for boys as well.

Sunset in a Fishing Village

On my raincape—ice; all over my body—frost;
at a fisher's shack on a mossy bank, wealth and rank
     have no end.
White haired, I sing vainly, poems broad as rivers
     and seas;
My tall fishing rod takes the light of the setting sun.

Foothills beneath
a deepening pall of snow
as twilight falls.

Far away in a cedar grove
the muffled boom of a bell.

Such a mind is, indeed,
that of a Buddha!

    The infant-child
is still free from drawing
    distinctions.

As darkness falls,
swollen with stormy winds
it spits the moon:
the looming peak of autumn
pines chill along the crest.

TR. ESPERANZA RAMIREZ-CHRISTENSEN

Without understanding,
would it not become a hindrance
    to the Dharma?

In the boat, observing the wind
In the drifting clouds at sea.

Cuckoo
[A one-hundred verse sequence, of which the last ten verses are given here]

1   In the swift current,
was that boat cast adrift upon
    the evening river?

2   The incessant sound of
waves pounding the shore.

3   Yellow mountain roses—
with each petal shower the water
    turns, colorless.

4   The eightfold dewdrops also
a hazy shimmer in sunlight.

5   The spring rain is
seeping finely over all,
    this morning.

6   A heart is breaking into shards
in wake of the dawn's parting.

7   Surely there are
worlds where one can live free
    of this yearning.

8   But how can I ever find
      the way to quiet my mind?

9   On moonlit nights, and
   even nights blotted of the moon,
       I lie disconsolate.

10   About the rice-warden's pallet,
     The chill of the wind deepens.

Invisible as the wind to the eye,
the mountain echo from the sky.

In everything
is and is-not are wholly
a matter of form.

Soul mad with longing
wanders off into the sky.

   A crow shrieks—
before the moon of a frosty night
   I lie alone.

"If it be so,
so be it!" Having said thus,
    why the hurry?

For the shadow trails the light,
implacably, indifferent to men.

A temporary lodging
on this side of the road all
must go, in the end.

To recover the time he rested,
The traveller hastens on.

SHINKEI

TR. ESPERANZA RAMIREZ-CHRISTENSEN

Spring

That man's life is but a dream—
Is what we now come to know.

Its house abandoned,
the garden has become home
    to butterflies.

TR. STEVEN CARTER

Summer

Just a hint of thunder clouds
    in the evening sky.
On summer mountains,
the faint disk of the moon—
night just beginning.

Autumn

Bushes bend toward earth
   before a snowy daybreak.

A storm passes
   and in the garden, moonlight—
night growing cold.

TR. STEVEN CARTER

Winter

Not a cloud around the moon
   in the sky at break of day.

Over my pillow,
it was rain showers and wind
   that ended my dream.

1   They come about on their own—
     the principles of all things.

     Water need not think
        to offer itself as lodging
           for clear moonlight.

2   Over rocks, a path toward
        a temple on a lone hill.

     Leaning on his staff,
     a pilgrim at his devotions
        is now old in years.

3   On which mountain
        of these covered with blossoms
           shall I seek lodging?

     For a bird kept in a cage—
     ah, the heartbreak of spring!

4   The pond—a sea;
     the branches—thick groves far back
        in summer hills.

5   Ah, for coolness
        it rivals the water's depths—
           this autumn sky.

Saying Goodbye to the Monk Wunian

Each five years we meet
then grieve when we must part.
It has taken only three farewells
for fifteen years to pass.
I recall how I tried to study meditation with you
but I was like the yellow poplar
    which grows for a while
        then shrinks again.
A hundred times I heard you lecture
but my mind remained a tangled knot.
I was like a man born blind
who has never seen red or purple—
try explaining the difference to him
and the more you speak
    the more confused he'll get.
I can't bear to leave you now
but it is impossible for us
    to stay together.
It is October—the river winds are blowing hard;
please let your hair grow back in
    to protect your head from the cold.

YUAN HONGDAO   201
TR. JONATHAN CHAVES

On Receiving My Letter of Termination

The time has come to devote myself to my hiker's stick;
I must have been a Buddhist monk in a former life!
Sick, I see returning home as a kind of pardon.
A stranger here—being fired is like being promoted.
In my cup, thick wine; I get crazy-drunk,
eat my fill, then stagger up the green mountain.
The southern sect, the northern sect, I've tried
    them all:
this hermit has his own school of Zen philosophy.

Writing Down What I See

The setting sun brings a pallor to the face of autumn;
floating clouds gather quickly into clusters.
They slant down, veiling the trees,
only two or three mountains still visible in the haze.
My horse glances back at the bridge-spanned river;
a group of monks returns along a path of pine trees.
The cliff is too high—I can see no temple;
suddenly, through the mist, I hear
    a temple bell.

1

On dead branches crows remain perched at
    autumn's end

2

Skull exposed in a field in my mind—the wind pierces
    my body

3

An old pond: a frog jumps in—the sound of water

4

Bright moon: strolling around the pond all night long

5

A cuckoo fades away, and in its direction, a single
    island

6

This autumn, why do I get old? In clouds a bird

1

The sea dark,
The call of the teal
Dimly white.

2

The beginning of art—
The depth of the country
And a rice-planting song.

3

Silent and still: then
Even sinking into the rocks,
The cicada's screech.

4

A flash of lightning:
Into the gloom
Goes the heron's cry.

1

On the mountain road the sun arose
Suddenly in the fragrance of plum-flowers.

2

[When visiting a Buddhist priest]

Quite unknown to the passers-by—
The chestnut-flowers by your house.

3

In his absence the god's garden
Is neglected, dead leaves piling.

4

Yield to the willow
All passions, all desires of your heart.

1

Coming this mountain way, no herb
Is lovelier than the violet.

2

A rough sea, and the Milky Way
Stretching across to Sado's isle.

3

Octopus pot, aye! and a brief dream
While the summer moon is shining.

4

Oh! skylark for whose carolling
The livelong day sufficeth not.

1   The whitebait
Opens its black eyes
    In the net of the Law.

2   A cloud of cherry blossoms:
The bell,—is it Ueno?
    Is it Asakusa?

3   *[On visiting a Zen master's temple after he
had died]*

      Even the woodpecker
Will not harm this hermitage
    Among the summer trees.

4   By daylight
The nape of the neck of the firefly
    Is red.

1   Asleep within the grave
     The soldiers dream, and overhead
        The summer grasses wave.

2   Nearing my journey's end,
     In dreams I trudge the wild waste moor,
        And seek a kindly friend.

3   A hundred years and more,
     Each year has cast its withered leaves
        My little garden o'er.

MATSUO BASHO   209
TR. WILLIAM PORTER

Priceless is one's incantation,
Turning a red-hot iron ball to butter oil.
Heaven? Purgatory? Hell?
Snowflakes fallen on the hearth fire.

TR. LUCIEN STRYK AND TAKASHI IKEMOTO

Past, present, future: unattainable,
Yet clear as the moteless sky.
Late at night the stool's cold as iron,
But the moonlit window smells of plum.

TR. LUCIEN STRYK AND TAKASHI IKEMOTO

You no sooner attain the great void
Than body and mind are lost together.
Heaven and Hell—a straw.
The Buddha-realm, Pandemonium—a shambles.
Listen: a nightingale strains her voice, serenading
    the snow.
Look: a tortoise wearing a sword climbs the lampstand.
Should you desire the great tranquillity,
Prepare to sweat white beads.

TR. LUCIEN STRYK AND TAKASHI IKEMOTO

My house is buried in the deepest recess of the forest.
Every year, ivy vines grow longer than the year before.
Undisturbed by the affairs of the world I live at ease,
Woodmen's singing rarely reaching me through
    the trees.
While the sun stays in the sky, I mend my torn clothes
And facing the moon, I read holy texts aloud to myself.
Let me drop a word of advice for believers of my faith.
To enjoy life's immensity, you do not need many
    things.

Green spring, start of the second month,
colors of things turning fresh and new.
At this time I take my begging bowl,
In high spirits tramp the streets of the town.
Little boys suddenly spot me,
delightedly come crowding round,
descend on me at the temple gate,
dragging on my arms, making steps slow.
I set my bowl on top of a white stone,
hang my alms bag on a green tree limb;
here we fight a hundred grasses,
here we hit the *temari* ball—
I'll hit, you do the singing!
Now I'll sing, your turn to hit!
We hit it going, hit it coming,
Never knowing how the hours fly.
Passers-by turn, look at me and laugh,
"What makes you act like this?"
I duck my head, don't answer them—
I could speak but what's the use?
You want to know what's in my heart?
From the beginning, just this! just this!

214   RYOKAN
TR. BURTON WATSON

I am imprisoned in my cottage among the solitary
     hills,
And think about the wet snow driving outside my
     window.
The cries of black monkeys are echoed by rocky
     summits.
The icy stream runs hushed at the bottom of the valley.
The flaming light by the window is chilled to its core,
And frost-dry is the ink-slab I have placed on my desk.
The night has thus prevented me from falling
     to repose.
I employ my brush, often warming it with my
     own breath.

RYOKAN

TR. NOBUYUKI YUASA

Begging food, I went to the city,
on the road met a wise old man.
He asked me, "Master, what are you doing
living there among those white-clouded peaks?"
I asked him, "Sir, what are you doing
growing old in the middle of this red city dust?"
We were about to answer, but neither had spoken
when fifth-watch bells shattered my dream.

At an old temple
In the depths of Takano
In the province of Ki,
I spend the night listening
To raindrops through the cedars.

Firm on the seven Buddhas' cushion,
Center, center. Here's the armrest
My master handed down. Now, to it!
Head up, eyes straight, ears in line with
shoulders.

Dogen

In the still night by the vacant window,
wrapped in monk's robe I sit in meditation,
navel and nostrils lined up straight,
ears paired to the slope of the shoulders.
Window whitens—the moon comes up;
rain's stopped, but drops go on dripping.
Wonderful—the mood of this moment—
distant, vast, known to me only!

My beloved friend
You and I had a sweet talk,
Long ago, one autumn night.
    Renewing itself,
The year has rumbled along,
That night still in memory.

RYOKAN   219
TR. NOBUYUKI YUASA

Good manners and sweet habits have faded,
 year after year.
Both court and country have sunk down,
 one age to another.
Men's hearts have grown stiff and stony,
 as time descends.
The First Teacher's steps have dimmed,
 after hard wearing.
Leaders of numerous sects cry out beliefs of their making.
Their disciples shout even louder to promote their causes.
Leaders and disciples alike stick together on their guard.
On peril of their lives, they do not yield to their enemy.
If, in religion, sects rule absolute, each in its dignity,
Who, amid the ancient saints, could not have taken a lead?
And if each man, in his own power, wishes to found a sect,
Alas, I know not where I might find a proper place for me.
Leaders of different sects, stay your quarrelling a while,
And bend your slow ears to what I have to say on
 my faith.
My faith has trickled down far away from its chief source;
Who preached at Mount Ryozen is whom I must
 first recommend.
He has climbed, beyond our reach, to the zenith of heaven.
No one alive has wisdom enough to know his right
 or wrong.
About five hundred years after he sank into
 eternal gloom,

Learned men began to interpret his teachings in
    many ways,
Until a great man was born unto this world, a guide to us,
Who sorted out problems and wove a subtle web
    of thinking.
He, moreover, acted out what he thought right in
    his view,
So again, no one can aspire to discuss his right or wrong.
By and by, my faith found its way into an eastern country,
Where its sole foundation was built at the temple,
    Hakuba.
Into this country came, through hardships, a wise teacher,
And placed under his leadership sects then in mortal feud.
It was during the well-governed reign of the
    T'ang Dynasty,
When the flowers of wisdom budded and bloomed
    all at once.
People listened to him and followed him with
    high respect.
He led the sects in full accord, like a lion in the woods.
Signs of disintegration were rank shortly after his death,
But the sad split between north and south came
    much later.
It was but in the last troublous days of the Sung Dynasty,
When the white wall of Zen tumbled to the pressure
    of men.
Then the so-called five schools began to lift their heads,

And they together opposed the proud eight sects
    for power.
The result was naught but confusion followed
    by confusion.
Alas, no one is alive now who can put it right by his wit.
My faith took root in my native land at the temple, Eihei,
Planted there by a man who rose by himself above
    the rest.
This man bore his master's seal far away from
    Mount Taihaku,
And founded his solid fame in my country,
    loud as thunder.
What he chose to teach in his books caused wonder
    and awe.
Even fierce elephants and dragons would have
    been quelled.
Many have walked along the highway of faith marked
    by him,
And arrived in the regions of pure light, lit by his fire.
His books are free from needless quibbles and repetitions,
And contain all we ever need to study about our salvation.
Alas, since the teacher left my country, this divine land,
I know not how many ages have slipped in quick
    succession;
During which time, weeds rose to oppress the house
    of Zen,
And herbs of fragrance have all drooped, unable to resist.

Who, amid the holies now, can move sun-warm lips
        like his,
When the cries of self-sacred divines daily tire the town?
I cannot arrest the surge of sorrow in my heart, for I am
A weak man come to the world to face its worst in history.
When the whole frame threatens to tumble down
        through rot,
How can I, a single man, carry its weight on my
        shoulders?
One quiet night, deprived of sleep, my eyes under a spell,
I rolled over many times in my bed, and wrote these lines.

Our life in this world—
to what shall I compare it?
It's like an echo
    resounding through the mountains
    and off into the empty sky.

You mustn't suppose
I never mingle in the world
Of humankind—
It's simply that I prefer
to enjoy myself alone.

RYOKAN
TR. DONALD KEENE

Since I began to climb this steep path of discipline,
I have lived behind a fast gate and a thousand hills.
Aged trees rise dark about me, fettered by ivy vines.
Rocks look cold on the hillsides, half-covered in clouds.
The posts of my house are all ruined by nightly rain,
My holy gown reduced to shreds by early morning
     mist.
No news of me my kin or the world have cared
     to know,
Year after year, for all the years I have lived here.

Foothills far below,
Mount Kugami soars to heaven.
    At its shady foot
Stands the shrine of Otogo.
    Here I live alone
Every morning and each night
    On the rugged rocks,
Or through the mossy footway,
    Coming and going
To perform my daily chores.
    Before me rises,
Each time I cast up my eyes,
    A primeval grove
Divine in its dark grandeur.
    Every year in May,
Cuckoos return from the south,
    And in noisy flocks
Swell their throats in ecstasy.
    When, in September,
Rain comes drizzling from above,
    Seated by the hearth
I tear off bright maple leaves.
    Thus for many years,
As long as life stays with me,
    Here I shall live free as air.

In the shady grove
Hopping light from twig to twig
    Cuckoos in a flock
Swell their throats in ecstasy,
Now that spring has crept away.

    Can I entice you
To rest your feet in my house?
    Over the foothills
Perhaps you will come gleaning
Red maple leaves all the way.

    Frosty maple leaves
Bright in their autumnal hues,
    And summer cuckoos,
I shall keep in mind for years
And years, until my life fails.

    Amid holy trees,
Close to the Otogo shrine,
    Seated all alone
I hear the sacred bells ring:
Perhaps, a call from a friend.

TR. NOBUYUKI YUASA

If anyone asks,
"How's that recluse?" I answer:
If the rain falls
   from the far sky, let it rain!
If the wind blows, let it blow!

RYOKAN
TR. STEVEN CARTER

The wind is gentle,
The moon is bright.
Come then, together
We'll dance the night out
As a token of old age.

230 RYOKAN
TR. GEOFFREY BOWNAS AND ANTHONY
THWAITE

Here are the ruins of the cottage where I once hid myself.
Revisited now in stark solitude, my cane alone at my side.
The fences have tumbled over the walks of foxes and hares.
The well has dried up, nearly covered over by rank bamboo.
Cobwebs hang slack at the window, where once I had a desk.
The floor I sat upon for long meditation has sunk in dust.
The garden steps have fallen under the bushy autumn grass.
Crickets alone raise their cries as if in defiance of man.
Loth to leave this place, I maunder around for many hours,
Till, appalled at the twilight, I watch the declining sun.

All my life too lazy to try and get ahead,
I leave everything to the truth of Heaven.
In my sack three measures of rice,
by the stove one bundle of sticks—
why ask who's got satori, who hasn't?
What would I know about that dust, fame and gain?
Rainy nights here in my thatched hut
I stick out my two legs any old way I please.

On the Death of Yukinori

Our life span, however long, lasts not for a hundred years,
And we all drift along through time like a boat in a river.
Our course has been determined by Karma, a chain of causes.
Few of us, though, are wise enough to take it into account.
When I was a boy, I had a couple of close friends about me.
We often played together on the banks of the Narrow Stream.
Already, literature was our concern, and we often sat down
In an earnest conversation, not caring how time crept away.
Among my friends, you were closest to me, and knew me best.
We went to school together, studied under the same teacher.
Many a morning, we followed each other on our way to class,
And having arrived, we sat down on the floor, side by side.
One day, however, a storm rose out of the dark to sever us.
We were then parted from each other, like heaven and earth.
You had in your mind a deep aspiration for worldly dignity.
I had in my heart a secret longing to follow ancient sages.
You went eastward, taking yourself beyond the Capital City.
I journeyed west to a holy temple in a province by the sea.
The west, however, was not my home, where I truly belonged.
Therefore, I tarried but a few seasons, and left the place.
After years of aimless wandering, I have at last come home,
Though I still live in the mountains under drifting clouds.
I seek shelter in a cottage, covered with a roof of pampas,
Standing apart halfway up on a shadowy slope of Mt. Kugami.
The home, however, is not the home I used to know long ago.

Each morning and every night, some change occurs
    somewhere.
Some time ago I met an acquaintance and inquired after you.
Instead of replying, he pointed out a grassy hillock to me.
When I knew what it was, my breath stopped, and I
    was dumb.
After moments of silence, tears swelled in spite of myself.
Once on a time, you were my bosom friend, studying
    with me.
Now you are imprisoned in a grave beneath the mossy
    ground.
It was my daily comfort to listen to your honeyed speeches.
Alas, we are now separated for ever as darkness from light.
How appallingly transitory are the three divisions of time!
How strangely undefinable are the six steps of our journey!
I took leave of the aged man who had told me of your death,
And walked out of the city on my cane, away from the noise.
On each side of the highway rose a line of evergreen pines,
And beyond them, roofs of large temples pierced the clouds.
Willow trees boasted of the flags fluttering in the breeze,
And roadside peaches dropped their flowers on gilt saddles.
For it was a market day, and busy swarms thronged the city,
And people marched along the highroad in a long
    procession.
I watched them with a steady gaze, cherishing a faint hope.
Alas, tears blinded my sight when I found no familiar face.

TR. NOBUYUKI YUASA

I have a walking stick—
don't know how many generations it's been handed
        down—
the bark peeled off long ago,
nothing left but a sturdy core.
In past years it tested the depth of a stream,
how many times clanged over steep rocky trails!
Now it leans against the east wall,
neglected, while the flowing years go by.

From Spring to Autumn of 1827 Some Things Came to Me Which I Wrote Down Haphazardly [no. 15 in a series]

I once wrote a poem swearing off poems;
it was 1820; the poem was wordy.

The most pressing things you want to say
have always been hard to say clearly.

So I'll try to say them with cunning words,
but before I can say them, my voice fails.

I seek no forgiveness from the gods,
and would even less speak it to living men.

To the east of a cloud, one scale exposed,
one claw is exposed on the other side.

But better than showing scale and claw
is to show no claw and scale at all.

More true still of the things I've said—
of scale and claw the lingering trace.

I repent my writings from the very first,
in heart's silence I will strive for Void.

This year I truly swear off poems—
The problem is not that my talent is gone.

A Renunciation of Wit

Buddhists tell of flames of Kalpa consuming all they
     meet;
Whence then rises this endless, angry tide of passion?
My days are frittered away in business and writing,
But at night come fitful fancies, subtle visions . . .
I draw my sword when thick and fast they press,
And with a flute dispel the last faint traces.
All palliatives, all wit, show a mind diseased;
I must burn my allegories by the lamp.

GONG ZIZHEN   237
TR. YANG XIANYI AND GLADYS YANG

BIOGRAPHIES

*Brief biographies of the poets in this anthology, in chrono-
logical order (some dates given are approximate or disputed)*

XIE LINGYUN (385–433). Scion of a wealthy and influ-
ential family in south China during the Six Dynasties,
Xie Lingyun was one of China's first and best-known
nature poets. He was strongly attracted to Buddhism
and to the idea of instantaneous enlightenment, appar-
ently influenced by the monk Zhu Daosheng (who is
sometimes portrayed as being a spiritual precursor of
Chan – Zen in China).

HUINENG (638–713). The sixth and most revered patri-
arch of Chan according to orthodox histories, Huineng
is said to have lived in the Nanhua temple north of
Guangzhou (Canton), where his mummified body was
later preserved. Little is known for certain about him,
though many legends grew up around him after his
death. His teachings are described in various versions
of *The Platform Sutra*.

WANG WEI (?701–761). Scion of a distinguished family,
Wang Wei is regarded as one of the finest Chinese poets
of the Tang dynasty (618–907), along with Du Fu, Li
Bai and Bai Juyi (see below for Bai). Wang Wei was
strongly drawn to Chan and other sects of Buddhism,
and wrote stele inscriptions for Huineng and the Chan

monk Daoguang. He wrote little overtly religious poetry, being remembered best for his nature poetry. Wang Wei was said to have been a remarkable painter as well as a poet, though none of his paintings has survived: the Song poet Su Dongpo declared that "in his poems there are paintings . . . in his paintings, poems".

LIU CHANGQING (710–85). A mid-Tang poet, Liu is best remembered for his nature poetry and poems reflecting disappointed political hopes.

HANSHAN (8th century). Hanshan, or Cold Mountain, was probably a recluse who took the name Cold Mountain from the place where he lived. What little we know about him is based on the 311 poems attributed to him in the *Complete Tang Poems*. Not all of these are by the same author, but most of them seem to be from the hand of one man, an eccentric personality of Buddhist, and to some extent Chan, persuasion. The Hanshan poems, though vivid, are not as well regarded as the work of men like Wang Wei, Du Fu or Li Bai; nonetheless Hanshan has come to be regarded as a central figure in Zen history and legend.

SHIDE (8th century). A close companion of Hanshan's, sometimes portrayed as a kind of alter ego, though in fact he is only mentioned once in Hanshan's poems.

SAMI MANZEI (8th century). Little is known about this Japanese priest, one of whose claims to fame is the often-quoted tanka (or short song) in this anthology.

CHANG JIAN (fl. 749). A Chinese poet of the mid-Tang of whom little is known; remembered mainly for his poetic descriptions of nature and religious sites.

JIAORAN (730–99). A Buddhist priest with a wordly disposition, Jiao Ran's lay surname was Xie, and he was the tenth generation descendant of Xie Lingyun. He ranked highly among Chinese Buddhist poets of the Tang dynasty, and is credited with being the first literary critic to point out common ground between Chan and artistic inspiration.

BAI JUYI (772–846). Also known as Bo Juyi (Bo being an older way of pronouncing his surname Bai), Bai Juyi was a mid-Tang poet of great versatility. He lived through troubled times, including an official attack on Buddhism that led to the closure of monasteries in 842–5. His own lifelong devotion to Buddhism was eclectic rather than relating to one particular sect. In his admiring biography of Bai the translator Arthur Waley remarked on Bai's extraordinary compassion, reflected in the tone of much of what he wrote, including his popular ballad, *The Song of Lasting Sorrow.*

LIU ZONGYUAN (773–819). Noted for his prose style, and especially his essays on landscapes, Liu was a Chinese scholar official who found solace in Buddhism but more as a Confucian than a strict adherent to Buddhist doctrine.

JIA DAO (779–845). A Buddhist monk early in life, Jia

Dao later returned to lay life to serve as an official. His evocative, often melancholy poetry influenced Chinese poets of the late Tang and Song dynasties.

GUANXIU (832–912). A poet, painter and Buddhist monk who lived in present-day Sichuan province in China, Guanxiu was called "Great Master of the Chan Moon" and highly regarded as a poet of exotic scenes. His reputation declined in the centuries after his death.

JIANZHANG (10th century). One of the so-called "Nine Monks", a group of Chinese Buddhist monk-poets active during the early years of the Song dynasty.

WEIFENG (10th century). Like Jianzhang, one of the "Nine Monks" of the early Song dynasty.

SU DONGPO, or SU SHI (1037–1101). Generally regarded as the greatest poet of the Song dynasty, an era in which urban Chinese lived lives that were strikingly modern in outlook, Su wrote on a wide range of subjects. He led the life of a scholar-official and had broad philosophical interests. Chan attracted a great deal of his attention, especially in his later years. Later, Zen monks in Japan treated Su Dongpo and his famous disciple Huang Tingjian not just as poetic inspirations but also as sources of Buddhist wisdom; Chinese critics have been more sceptical about this latter aspect of their work. Su's given name was Shi; he started calling himself Dongpo ("Eastern Slope") in his forties, after a plot of land he farmed.

CHEN SHIDAO (1052–1102). A friend of Su Dongpo's, Chen was a poor man from a commoner's family, and found official employment with Su's help. A member of the Jiangsu school of poets in east China, he was a Buddhist devotee and took the name of Hou Shan Jushi ("Lay Buddhist of the Back Hills").

SAIGYO (1118–90). A Buddhist priest, Saigyo's life straddled the Heian and Kamajura periods in Japanese history. He is one of the best-loved poets in Japan. Part of his enduring appeal may be his rare combination of worldly scepticism and other-worldly seclusiveness. Saigyo was not a Zen priest; he belonged to the Shingon or Mantra school of Buddhism: but as with many such poets, the Zen mood of his writings transcends sectarian boundaries.

FAN CHENDA (1126–93). A Chinese scholar-official whose poetry sometimes reflected Buddhist sentiments though his world view was broadly Confucian. Fan is regarded as one of the "Four Masters" of poetry of the southern Song dynasty, his poetry best known for its contemplation of nature and the countryside. Like Yang Wanli (see below), he was influenced as a poet by Chan concepts of enlightenment applied to art.

YANG WANLI (1127–1206). Yang led the life of a Chinese scholar official in troubled times. One of the "Four Masters" of the southern Song, he was a highly productive poet and had a lifelong interest in Chan, which grew stronger in old age. Throughout his life Yang compared artistic enlightenment – we would say genius – to the enlightenment of Chan, and saw the two processes in the same light. "Get rid of words and meaning," he once wrote, "and there is still poetry." In 1178 he claimed he experienced a sudden enlightenment, and went on to write what most people think is his best work.

JAKUREN (1139–1202). A Japanese Buddhist priest who led a worldly life in court and at the capital during the early part of the Kamakura period.

MYOE (1173–1232). A Japanese priest of the Kegon (Hua Yan, Flowery Splendour) school of Buddhism, which together with Zen was one of the main schools of Buddhism at the time. Myoe had a reputation as a crazy eccentric, and after his death was portrayed as a pious recluse.

KIGEN DOGEN (1200–53). A leading Buddhist thinker and religious leader during the early Kamakura period, Dogen spent four years in China then returned to Japan to establish the Soto Zen sect, one of the two or three main sects of Japanese Zen. Dogen's poems are read now largely because of his standing as a Zen master, rather than because of their literary merit.

KOKAN SHIREN (1278–1345). A scholar and poet of the Rinzai sect of Zen, which together with the Soto sect was one of the main sects of Zen at the time, Kokan

Shiren was an early representative of the Gozan or Five Mountain establishment (see Foreword).

JAKUSHITSU GENKO (1290–1367). A Five Mountain monk born of a noble family, Jakushitsu spent five years in China at the same time as Sesson Yubai (see below), but with fewer mishaps. On his return to Japan he led a quiet life in out-of-the-way temples, turning down more than one offer to become an abbot in the capital, Kyoto.

SESSON YUBAI (1290–1346). A Five Mountain monk, Sesson Yubai spent twenty-one years studying in China before returning to high religious office in Japan. At one point he was imprisoned in China by the Mongols, then rulers of the empire, and escaped execution only by giving a virtuoso display of Chan poetic composition. Later he was exiled to Shu (present-day Sichuan province in China), where he wrote a number of poems that are now his only surviving poetic work.

BETSUGEN ENSHI (1294–1364). A Five Mountain monk who spent ten years in China, unhappily to judge from the discontented poetry he wrote there.

PAEGUN (1299–1375). A master of Son (Zen in Korea), Paegun lived during the time of Mongol domination of Korea, in the last years of the Koryo dynasty.

CHUGAN ENGETSU (1300–75). A Five Mountain monk, Chugan was abandoned as a child and led a life punctuated by misfortune. He spent seven years in China, then returned to Japan in 1332, where he spent years in the provinces before becoming the abbot of one of the Zen temples in Kyoto.

RYUSEN REISAI (d. 1360). A Five Mountain monk, and the illegitimate son of the emperor Go-Daigo.

T'AEGU (1301–82). Like Paegun, National Preceptor T'aegu was a master of Son in Korea during the time of the Mongols.

RYUSHU SHUTAKU (1308–88). A Five Mountain monk, Ryushu was a famous calligrapher and painter, and seems to have suffered frequent illness, judging from the number of poems he wrote on the subject.

NAONG (1320–76). Royal Preceptor Naong was a Son master during the last years of the Koryo dynasty in Korea.

GIDO SHUSHIN (1325–88). Gido has had high standing among the Five Mountain monk poets of Japan. A sociable man, much of his poetry is courtly in tone, and apparently unconnected with Zen. Gido suffered from bad sight, perhaps cataracts, and used to emphasize how his poor sight enabled him to perceive the illusory nature of reality.

ZEKKAI CHUSHIN (1336–1405). A friend of Gido Shushin's, but more antisocial by nature, Zekkai Chushin spent ten years in China and had the rare privilege of an audience with the Chinese emperor (Taizu of the Ming dynasty). He returned to Japan in 1378 to find it in a state of civil unrest, but eventually held high office as a

Five Mountains abbot in Kyoto. The shogun at the time is said to have taken to Zekkai Chushin only gradually, disliking him at first but ending up by wearing his Zen robes into battle.

IKKYU SOJUN (1394–1481). A Zen Buddhist monk who is supposed to have been eccentric even by the standards of Zen at the time.

SHINKEI (1406–75). One of the most brilliant practitioners of renga (Japanese linked poetry), Shinkei was a Buddhist monk strongly influenced by Zen, even if it is not clear whether he ever affiliated himself with a Zen sect. In a famous comment, he wrote, "If you were to ask one of the great poets of the past how to compose waka [Japanese poetry], the answer would be pampas grass on a withered moor and the moon disappearing into the sky at dawn." In his later years he spent much of his time travelling, during a period when Japan was in turmoil as a result of the decade-long Onin War.

SOGI (1421–1502). Another renga master, Sogi survived the Onin War to become the most admired poet of his age. Trained as a Zen monk, he spent time as a mendicant priest before settling in Kyoto, where he achieved fame and glory as a writer, critic and poet.

YUAN HONGDAO (1568–1610). Not very well known outside China, Yuan Hongdao was the most famous of three literary brothers in the late Ming dynasty. Highly regarded as a poet and writer, he was influenced by

Chan Buddhism as well as being attracted to popular novels, plays and verse. He advocated a spontaneous literary style, breaking with what he saw as the stultifying conventions of the time.

MATSUO BASHO (1644–94). Commonly known as Basho, Japan's best-known and best-loved author. Basho led the life of a wandering hermit, and took his name from a series of "banana huts" (*basho an*) in which he lived at successive points in his life. He wrote several fine travel diaries, and was a master of hokku, the three-line opening stanza of a renga, consisting of 5, 7 and 5 syllables respectively (and nowadays called haiku). The Basho poems in this anthology are of this type. Basho's name is often associated with Zen, but while his work was influenced by Zen, the cryptic qualities of hokku, in Basho's and others' hands, reflect some of the qualities of traditional Japanese poetry, rather than Zen as such.

HAKUIN (1685–1768). A Japanese poet, painter and calligrapher of the Rinzai sect of Zen, Hakuin was the author of a number of famous *koan* (riddles), including the most famous of all, "the sound of one hand clapping".

RYOKAN (1758–1831). An unconventional and retiring poet, Ryokan became a monk of the Soto sect of Zen at an early age, and led an austere, unassuming life, whimsically giving himself the name of "Great Fool". In his old age he formed a close attachment to a young nun,

Teishin, who brought out the first selection of his poems, which up till then had remained unpublished. Many now regard him as the finest poet of his age.

GONG ZIZHEN (1792–1841). A Chinese official of reformist bent who failed in politics but succeeded in literature. Gong Zizhen eventually embraced Buddhism, and his writings are suffused by Chan language and metaphors.

ACKNOWLEDGMENTS

Thanks are due to the following copyright holders for their permission to reprint the following translations in this anthology:

BLYTH, R.H.: 'The whitebait' by Matsuo Basho, from *Volume One: Eastern Culture*, Hokuseido Press, Tokyo, 1981. BOWNAS, GEOFFREY, AND THWAITE, ANTHONY: 'Trailing on the wind', 'The winds of spring', 'Every single thing', by Saigyo; 'The sea dark' by Matsuo Basho; 'The wind is gentle' by Ryokan, from *The Penguin Book of Japanese Verse*, Penguin Books, 1964. Translation copyright © Geoffrey Bownas and Anthony Thwaite, 1964. Reproduced by permission of Penguin Books Ltd. BYNNER, WITTER: 'In my Lodge at Wang-chuan after a Long Rain', 'Lines', by Wang Wei; 'On Parting with the Buddhist Pilgrim Lingche' by Lui Changqing; 'At Wang Changling's Retreat' by Chang Jian, from *The Jade Mountain – A Chinese Anthology*, Anchor Books, New York, 1964. CARTER, STEVEN D.: 'If anyone asks', 'Our life in this world', by Ryokan; 'That man's life is but a dream', 'Just a hint of thunder clouds', 'Bushes bend towards the earth', 'Not a cloud around the moon', 'They come about on their own', by Sogi; 'Sunset in a Fishing Village', 'Like dew that vanishes', by Ikkyu Sojun; 'Imitating the Old Style' by Chugan Engetsu; 'Depending on Neither Words nor Letters', 'Worship Service', by Kigen Dogen; 'On seeing the First Bloom of the Lotus' by Jakuren. Reprinted from *Traditional Japanese Poetry: An Anthology*, translated, with an introduction, by Stephen D. Carter, with the permission of the publishers, Stanford University Press. © 1991 by the Board of Trustees of the Leland Stanford Junior University. CHAVES, JONATHAN: 'On Receiving My Letter of Termination', 'Writing Down What I See', 'Saying Goodbye to the Monk Wunian', by Yuan Hongdao, from *Pilgrim of the Clouds: poems and essays by Yuan Hüng-tao and His Brothers*, Weatherhill, New York and Tokyo, 1978; 'The Twin Pagodas of Orchid Stream', ' Don't Read Books!', 'Staying Overnight at Xiaosha Stream', 'Rising Early', 'The Cold Lantern', 'Passing the Pavilion on Shenzhu Bridge', 'Red Peonies in a Jar', 'The Boatman's Flute', by Yang Wanli, from *Heaven my Blanket, Earth my Pillow – Poems by Yang Wan-li*, Weatherhill, New York and Tokyo, 1975. CHAMBERLAIN, BASIL HALL: 'Coming this mountain way, no herb' by Matsuo Basho, from *An Anthology of Haiku Ancient and Modern*, Maruzen Co. Ltd., Tokyo, 1932. Reprinted by permission of Maruzen Co. Ltd. CHING TI: 'At Yiye Temple', 'A